English for Banking and Finance

Lorin Watt
McGraw - Hill Book Co.
71A Methonis str.
106 83 Athens Greece
Tel. 363.2722
Tlx: 214040

INSTRUMENTAL ENGLISH

English for Banking and Finance

David M. Stillman

Ronni L. Gordon

McGraw-Hill
New York St. Louis San Francisco Auckland Bogotá Guatemala Hamburg
Johannesburg Lisbon London Madrid Mexico Montreal New Delhi
Panama Paris San Juan São Paulo Singapore Sydney Tokyo Toronto

Editorial Development:

Senior Editor: Laurie Likoff
Associate Editor: Patricia Shaw
Design: Catherine Gallagher
Photo Research: Alice Lundoff
Illustrator: Heidi King

Library of Congress Cataloging in Publication Data

Stillman, David M.
　Instrumental English : English for banking and finance.

　1. English language—Text-books for foreigners.
2. English language—Business English.　3. Banks and banking—Terminology.　4. Finance—Terminology.
I. Gordon, Ronni L.　　II. Title.
PE1128.S78 1982　　　428.2'4'08865　　　82-13077
ISBN 0-07-004524-0

1 2 3 4 5 6 7 8 9 10　DODO　8 9 2 1 0 9 8 7 6 5 4 3

Copyright © 1983 by McGraw-Hill, Inc. All Rights Reserved.
Printed in the United States of America. No part of this publication may be reproduced, stored in a retrieval system, or transmitted, in any form or by any means, electronic, mechanical, photocopying, recording, or otherwise, without the prior written permission of the publisher.

**For Alexander Theodore
and Miriam Bess**

Picture Credits:

Permission to reprint the following pictures is hereby gratefully acknowledged:

Page xiv	©Jan Jachniewicz, The Chase Manhattan Bank
Page 8	NCR Corporation
Page 18	©William Devine, Chase Manhattan Bank
Page 26	©Arthur Lavine, The Chase Manhattan Bank
Page 38	©Glyn Cloyd
Page 50	©Raymond Juschkus, The Chase Manhattan Bank
Page 60	The Chase Manhattan Bank
Page 72	Courtesy, The Chicago Board of Trade
Page 80	©Glyn Cloyd
Page 90	©Jim Theologos
Page 100	©Edward C. Topple, courtesy New York Stock Exchange
Page 112	©Helaine Messer, courtesy Christie's Auctioneers, NY
Page 126	The Chase Manhattan Bank
Page 140	©Glyn Cloyd

CONTENTS

1. Savings Banks   1
   present tense—negatives, questions
   past tense—negatives, questions
2. Checking Accounts   9
   irregular past tense forms
   Reading Plus—advertisement for N.O.W. accounts
3. Loans   19
   more irregular past tense forms
   combining sentences: sentences with two clauses
4. Mortgages   27
   present perfect
   formation of the past participles
   Reading Plus—brochure about mortgages
5. Consumer Credit   39
   direct and indirect objects
   direct and indirect objects in the same sentence
   clauses as direct objects
   Reading Plus—credit card application
6. Wills and Estates   51
   passive voice
7. The Accounting Department   61
   uncountables
8. The Federal Reserve System   73
   indirect objects as subjects of **passive sentences**
9. International Banking Facilities   81
   future tense
   be + **going to** + simple verb
   Reading Plus—table of exchange rates
10. The International Monetary Fund   91
    comparison of adjectives and adverbs

11. Investments (Part I)   101
    negative and indefinite words
    Reading Plus—*New York Times* stock listings
12. Investments (Part II)   113
    modals
    Reading Plus—magazine advertisement
13. Electronic Banking   127
    conditional
    conditional sentences
    Reading Plus—automatic teller machine brochure
14. Devaluation   141
    adjective clauses
    infinitives and infinitive phrases with subjects

Appendix—numbers and dates   153

Vocabulary   155

Preface

Instrumental English for Banking and Finance has been written for the student of English who works in the sphere of banking and finance. This textbook is designed to give the student an introduction to English banking and financial terminology, while at the same time reviewing some of the more important grammatical structures of the language.

The book is divided into two sections of seven lessons each. The first section covers basic banking procedures; the second section deals with investment, and international banking and finance. This broad range of topics should meet the English language needs of people working across the whole spectrum of banking. An appendix of numbers and dates has also been provided as a reference for the student.

Each of the fourteen chapters of this book is centered on a different aspect of banking or finance, and provides numerous exercises, both structural and communicative, in which the learner practices the new vocabulary and grammatical points introduced in the lesson. Some lessons also contain supplementary readings (the *Reading Plus* sections) which give the student the opportunity to read authentic materials written in the field. Special emphasis has been given to international banking and international monetary arrangements in selecting topics for this book, in order to better meet the varied needs of our students.

We hope that *Instrumental English for Banking and Finance* will address those students of English who want to review and expand their command of the basic patterns of the language, while at the same time acquiring vocabulary that is closely related to their professional interests and concerns. This book will give them the knowledge and skills they need to use English successfully in the areas of banking and finance, and will provide them with a solid basis for more advanced study.

David M. Stillman, Ph.D.

Ronni L. Gordon, Ph.D

Harvard University Extension

Acknowledgments

We wish to thank the people who gave so generously of their time to advise us about various aspects of banking and finance and who helped gather materials that were indispensable in the preparation of this text.

They are Mr. Julius H. Stillman of Bankers Trust, New York; Dr. Robert I. Greene, Second Vice-President, Chase Manhattan Bank, New York; Mr. Harold W. Shankle, manager, Brookline Savings Bank, Brookline, Massachusetts. The support and information they provided were essential in enabling us to bring our project to its successful conclusion.

D.M.S.

R.L.G.

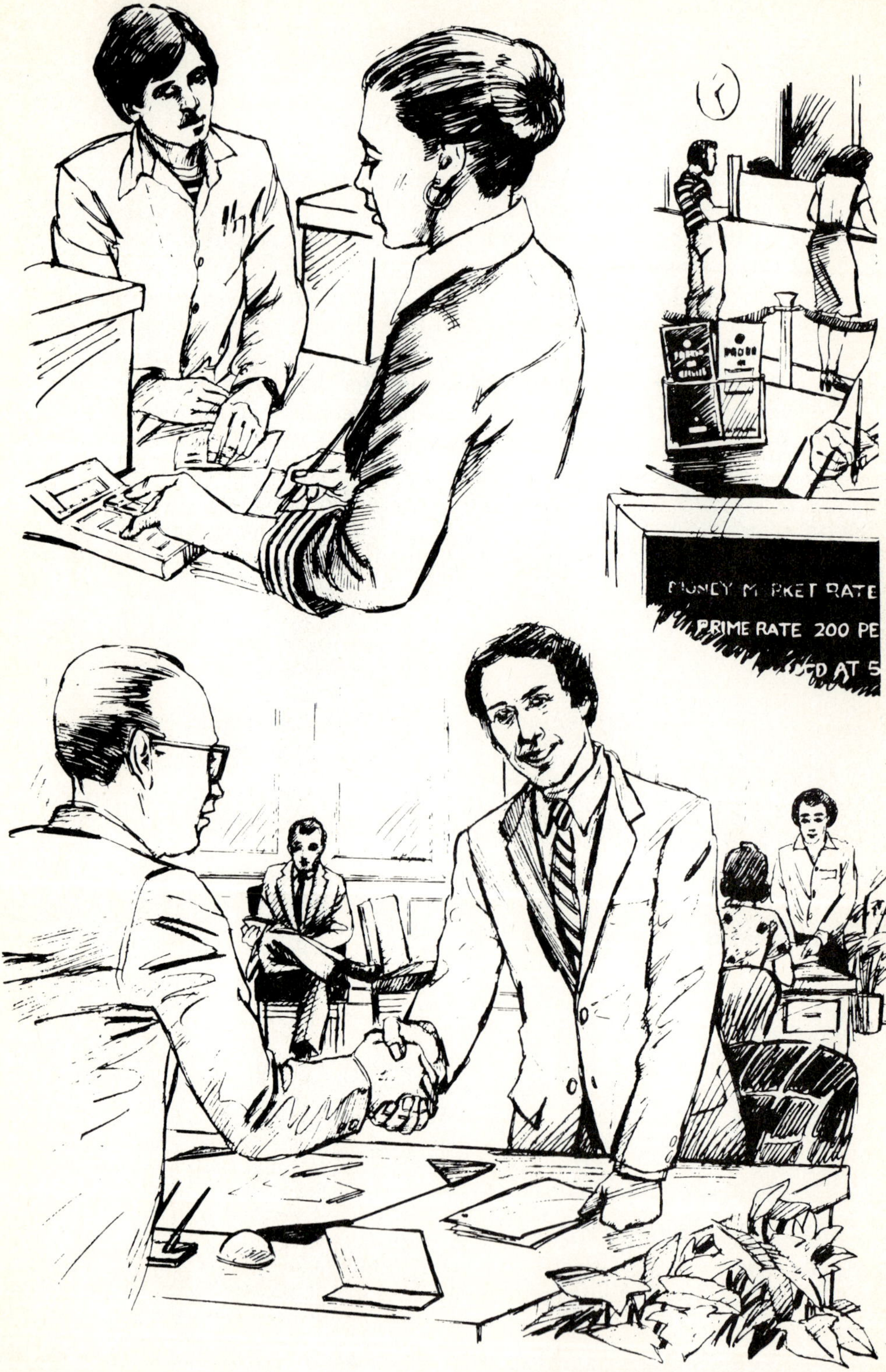
PRIME RATE 200 PE

PART I
BANKING SERVICES AND PROCEDURES

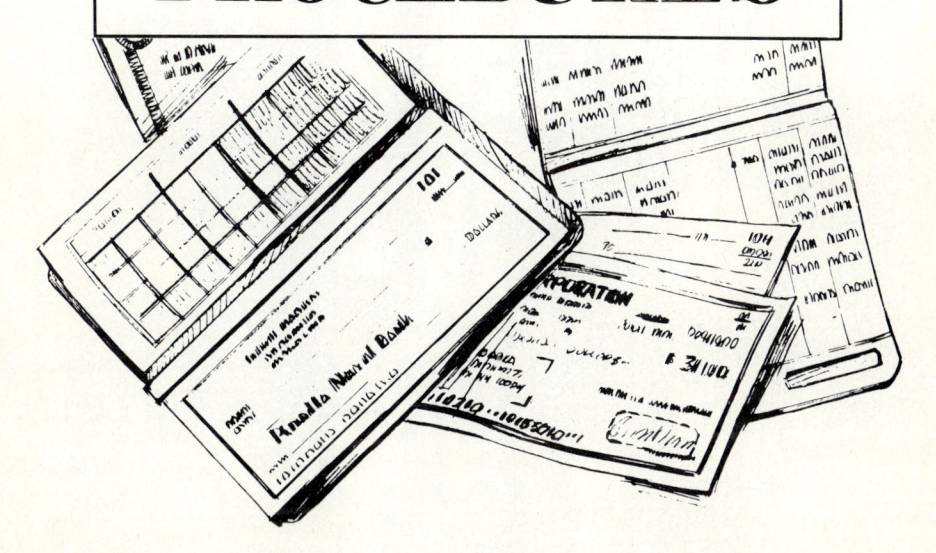

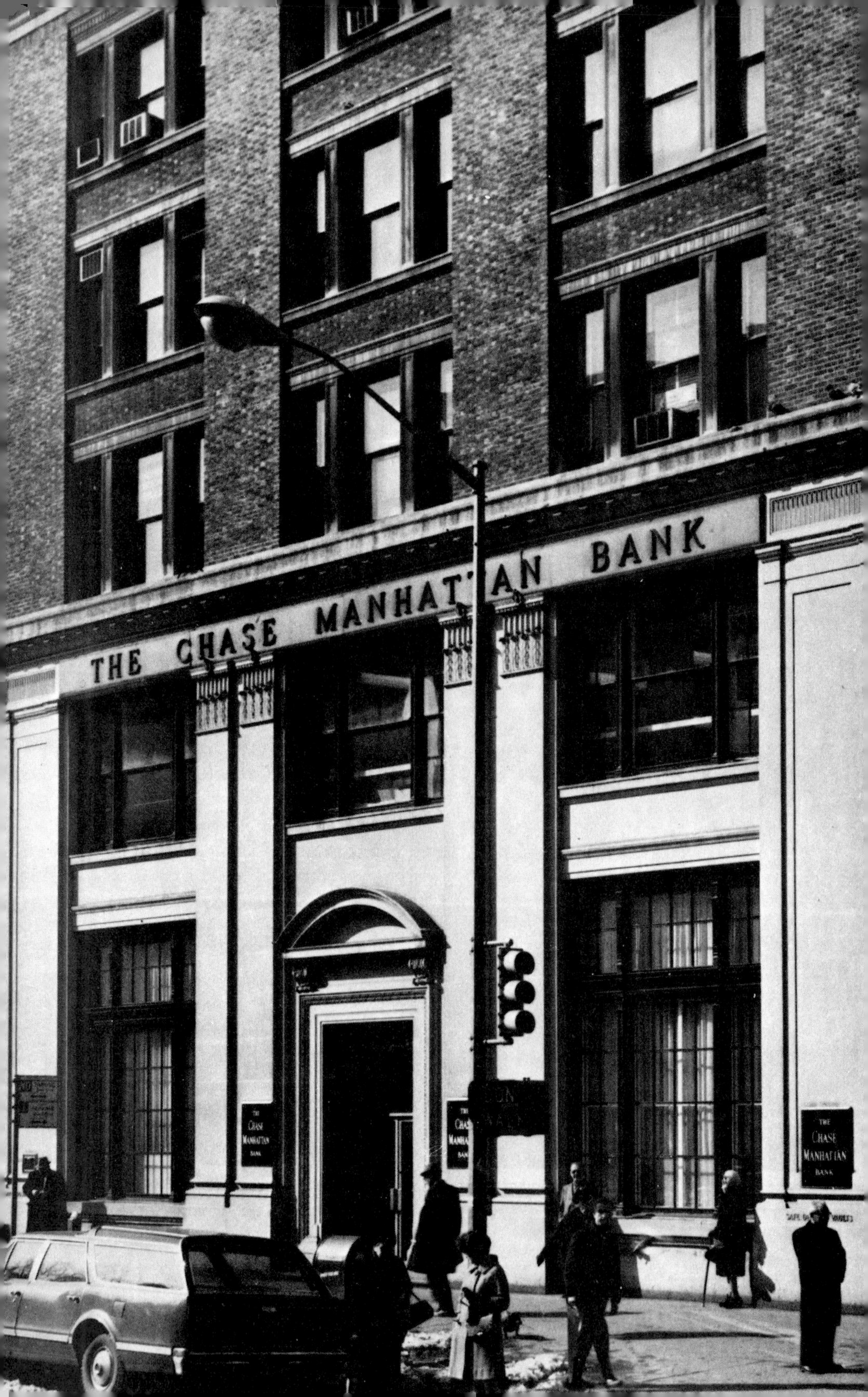
THE CHASE MANHATTAN BANK
THE CHASE MANHATTAN BANK

LESSON 1

SAVINGS BANKS

VOCABULARY

manager—person who directs or conducts the operations of a bank
paycheck—check for salary given by an employer to someone who works for him
window—the place where bank customers come to give money to or get money from a teller
to deposit—to put money into the bank
to withdraw—to take money out of the bank
  a deposit—money that a customer puts into the bank
  a withdrawal—money that a customer takes out of the bank
  a depositor—a customer of a bank who has an account there
a slip—a bank form used to order a deposit or withdrawal when filled out by the customer
teller—the person who receives and gives out money in a bank
to endorse—to write one's name on the back of a check in order to cash or deposit it
passbook—a small book that records a depositor's account. It shows her deposits, withdrawals and interest payments by the bank.
account—a statement or record of money that the bank owes a depositor; a record of a depositor's deposits and withdrawals
  a savings account—money left in the bank that draws interest
  a joint account—an account shared by two (or more) depositors
  a term-deposit account—an account in which the depositor agrees not to withdraw his money for a period of time
  to open an account—to begin depositing one's money in a bank
  to close an account—to withdraw all of one's money from the bank
interest—payment by the bank for the use of a depositor's money
party—one of the people interested in a contract; one of the depositors in a joint account
delay—slowness; lateness

1

Expansion

to fill out—to write the necessary information
  If you want to deposit money you have to fill out a **deposit slip**.
  If you want to withdraw money you have to fill out a **withdrawal slip**.
to sign—to write one's name
  Please sign on the last line of the slip.
signature—a person's name written by himself
  The bank requires the depositor's signature for all withdrawals.
rate—amount or percentage (%)
  "What is the current rate of interest on savings accounts?"
  "The bank pays 5 1/2% interest a year."
  Term-deposit accounts pay higher interest **rates** than regular **savings** accounts.
computer—an electronic machine that does difficult mathematical **operations** and that has a memory
  Modern banking depends on computers to perform (= do) complex operations.
to accommodate—to take care of, attend to, help
  There was a delay in accommodating the customers because the computer broke down.
assets—everything that a company or bank owns and that has value (= worth)
  current assets—assets that can be turned readily into cash
  fixed assets—land, buildings, equipment
  The assets of our bank are over $10,500,000.
liabilities—money owed by a company or bank
balance sheet—a statement of a company's assets and liabilities
to owe—to have to pay money
solvent—being able to pay all money that you owe
  Since his firm's assets equal the liabilities, his firm is solvent.

Vocabulary Practice

Select the answer that correctly completes each sentence.

1. An account that two or more people hold is a _____.
    a. joint account   b. term-deposit account   c. savings account
2. In order to withdraw money the bank requires your _____.
    a. depositor   b. interest   c. signature
3. The bank records all transactions of an account in the customer's _____.
    a. withdrawal slip   b. assets   c. passbook
4. Many banks work with so many different customers and accounts that they need _____ to record all transactions.
    a. deposit slips   b. computers   c. parties
5. You have to _____ your check in order to cash it.
    a. withdraw   b. endorse   c. accommodate

A BANK MANAGER SPEAKS

My name is Jane Carson and I'm the manager of a savings bank in Portland, Oregon. My bank is open every day from 8:30 in the morning until 4:00 in the afternoon. On Fridays the bank remains open until 6:30 in the evening.

Friday is our busiest day. Many people get their paychecks on Fridays and they come in to deposit them. I find that on Fridays I have to keep six windows open all day long. My bank tries very hard to reduce the amount of time that customers have to wait for service. We have many signs to remind people that they need their passbooks for all transactions and that they must fill out their deposit or withdrawal slips completely. If our depositors cooperate with us we can accommodate them with as few delays as possible.

Of course, people do forget. The tellers inform me that many customers still forget to endorse their checks or try to open or close joint accounts with the signature of only one of the parties. But I hope that my program of information for customers will reduce such delays.

Banking has changed a lot in recent years. Computers now do much of the work that the tellers used to do. As computers improve, they are able to accomplish more difficult tasks and they help us serve our customers better.

Another important change in banking, especially for savings banks, are the many different term-deposit accounts that are now available to our customers. Since these certificates of deposit offer very high interest rates they help attract depositors to our bank. I make sure that my staff always has the latest information about these accounts so that they can advise our depositors correctly.

My bank is not a very large bank. The total of our current assets and fixed assets comes to 15,550,000 dollars.[1] I'm proud of our balance sheet. Although some banks across the country are having difficulties, my bank has more assets than liabilities. We are solvent and growing. The number of customers we serve has increased this year and I expect that it will continue to grow in the future.

---

[1] Students needing a review of numbers should consult the Appendix.

Comprehension Check

A. State whether each sentence is true or false based on the reading.

1. Jane Carson's bank closes at 3:00 P.M. on Fridays.
2. Fridays are very busy days at Jane Carson's bank.
3. Ms. Carson has an information program for customers.
4. Computers and term-deposit accounts have brought changes to banks.
5. Jane Carson's bank has more liabilities than assets.

B. Answer the following questions orally.

1. What does a bank manager do?
2. How many windows are open on Fridays?
3. Why do they need so many windows on Fridays?
4. What are some of the ways in which customers cause delays?
5. What does a depositor have to do to open or close a joint account?
6. Why are computers important to a bank?
7. How do term-deposit accounts help a bank get new customers?
8. Why does the bank manager want her staff to have the latest information on term-deposit accounts?
9. How much money does Jane Carson's bank have in assets?
10. Why is Ms. Carson hopeful about the future of her bank?

C. Composition. Make a list of the most important aspects of Jane Carson's job.

Building Your Vocabulary

A. Matching. Find the words in the right-hand column that match the words closest in meaning in the left-hand column.

1. percentage
2. customer of a bank
3. person's written name
4. money owed
5. two-party account
6. director
7. piece of paper
8. money in the bank
9. record (noun)
10. lateness

a. savings
b. joint account
c. rate
d. slip
e. delay
f. account
g. manager
h. depositor
i. signature
j. liabilities

B. Rewriting sentences. Rewrite each of the following sentences replacing the underlined word or words with the correct form of one of the new words of this lesson.

Model: Please <u>write the necessary information on</u> this form.
   → Please fill out this form.
1. Please <u>write your name on</u> this slip.
2. The bank tries to <u>take care of</u> all its depositors.
3. I must <u>take out</u> fifty dollars today.
4. Please <u>sign the back of</u> this check.
5. Which bank offers a higher <u>percentage</u> of interest?

PRESENTATION

I. Present tense—negatives, questions

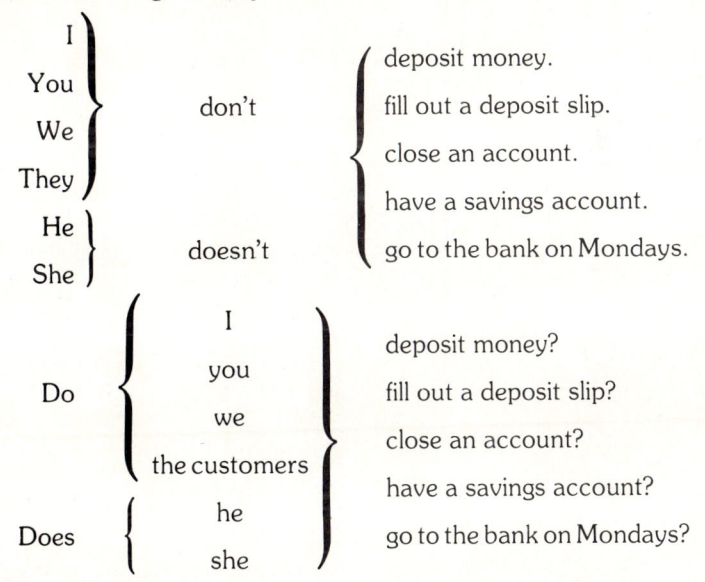

I, You, We, They	don't	deposit money.
		fill out a deposit slip.
		close an account.
		have a savings account.
He, She	doesn't	go to the bank on Mondays.

Do	I, you, we, the customers	deposit money?
		fill out a deposit slip?
		close an account?
		have a savings account?
Does	he, she	go to the bank on Mondays?

Structure Practice

A. Make each sentence negative by adding *don't* or *doesn't*.

Model: Mary works in a bank.
   → Mary doesn't work in a bank.
1. I deposit my paycheck on Fridays.
2. The customer endorses his check.
3. We fill out a deposit slip.
4. The manager helps you open an account.
5. We save a lot of money.

B. Now make each of the statements of exercise A into questions using *do* or *does*.

Model: Mary works in a bank.
   → Does Mary work in a bank?

II. Past tense—negatives and questions

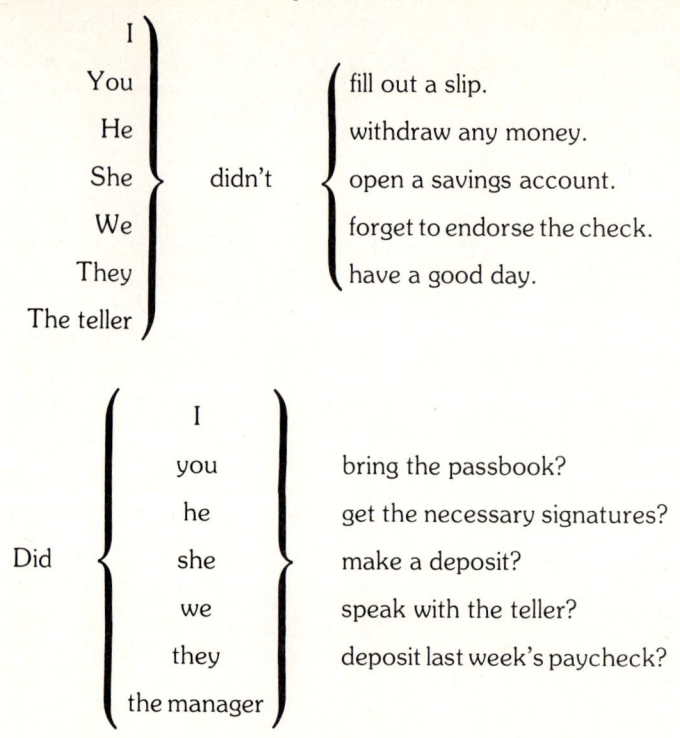

I / You / He / She / We / They / The teller } didn't { fill out a slip. / withdraw any money. / open a savings account. / forget to endorse the check. / have a good day.

Did { I / you / he / she / we / they / the manager } bring the passbook? / get the necessary signatures? / make a deposit? / speak with the teller? / deposit last week's paycheck?

Structure Practice

C. Make the following sentences negative using *didn't*. Remember to change the form of the verb from past to infinitive.

    Model: Mary worked in a bank.
            → Mary didn't work in a bank.
1. The customer deposited a lot of money.
2. Mrs. Allen closed her account.
3. The depositor endorsed his paycheck.
4. Mr. Robinson's wife signed the slip.
5. The computers caused a delay.

D. Now make each of the statements of exercise A into questions using *did*.

    Model: Mary worked in a bank.
            → Did Mary work in a bank?

Building Sentences

A. Select elements from columns **A**, **B** and **C** to make at least five sentences. Be sure that the sentences you form make sense.

A	B	C
Mrs. Allen	tried to	open a savings account.
The tellers	wanted to	accommodate all the customers.
The manager	forgot to	fill out the slip.
A depositor		close two of the windows.
		endorse his paycheck.

B. Replace forms of *want to* with the corresponding forms of *feel like* and make all necessary changes.

Model: I want to go home.
   → I feel like going home.
1. I want to work on Saturday.
2. Those depositors want to see the manager.
3. He doesn't want to go to the bank.
4. Mrs. Allen doesn't want to wait long.
5. The tellers want to rest this weekend.

C. Replace *must* by *'d better* or *had better*.

Model: You must speak to the manager.
   → You'd better speak to the manager.
1. They must fix the computers.
2. You must open a new account.
3. They must accommodate all their customers.
4. The bank must raise its interest rates.
5. The manager must open two more windows.

BANKING CONVERSATIONS

You work in a bank in the United States. Using the new vocabulary of this lesson, explain to a customer what he or she has to do in order to:
1. withdraw money
2. cash a check
3. close a joint account

Now explain the following things to a customer:
1. why there is a delay
2. what a teller does
3. which type of account pays higher interest rates

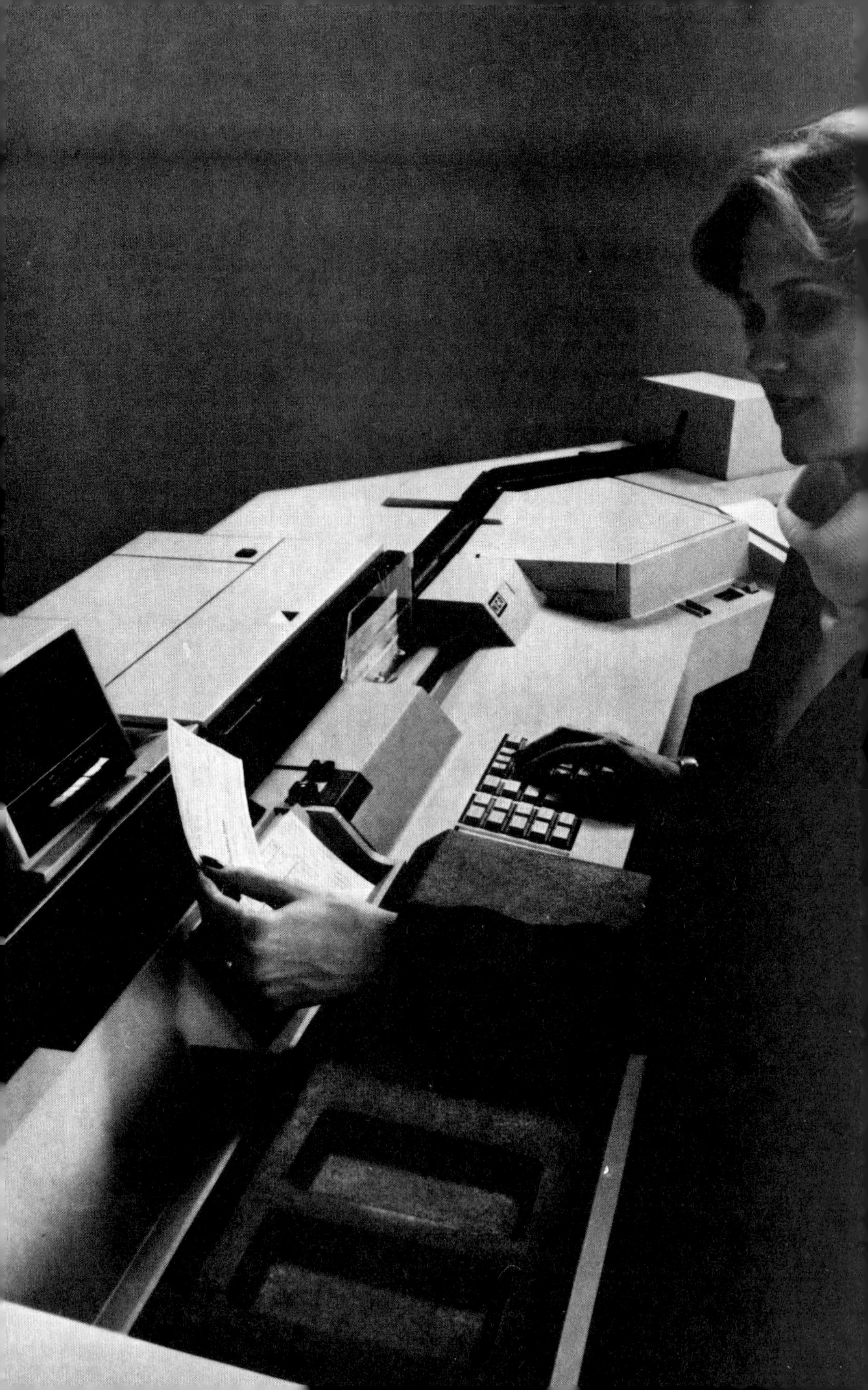

LESSON 2

CHECKING ACCOUNTS

VOCABULARY

checking account—funds that a customer has on deposit. He uses this money to pay the checks that he writes.

demand deposit—a customer can withdraw the money in a demand deposit without waiting for a period of time

commercial bank—a bank chartered by the national government or a state government (in the U.S.). Commercial banks specialize in loans and demand deposits, and serve business and industry.

fee—money paid for a service

transaction—a business deal, arrangement, or activity

record—a written account serving as a reminder or as evidence of a transaction

bookkeeping—systematic recording of business transactions

to administer—to be in charge of, direct, manage

service charge—a fee that a bank gets from a depositor for the bookkeeping involved in administering a depositor's account

monthly statement—a record that the bank sends each month to checking account holders that lists all checks that the bank has paid and all deposits that the customer has made

balance—money remaining in an account after checks are paid

minimum balance—a sum of money that the customer must keep in his account to avoid paying a service charge

outstanding check—a check that the depositor has written but which has not yet been presented for payment (= not yet been cashed)

stop payment—a request that a depositor makes to her bank. She asks the bank not to pay a check that she has already written.

overdrawn—a depositor is overdrawn when he writes a check for more money than he has in his account

penalty—a sum of money collected as a punishment for overdrawing an account

N.O.W. account—negotiable order of withdrawal account
   negotiable—said of an instrument such as a check that may be transferred to a third party
   order—written instructions to buy, sell or pay

Expansion

to keep the books—to maintain written records of business transactions
   When my firm was small I could keep the books myself.
cancelled check—a check that the bank has already paid and recorded in the depositor's account. These checks are marked "paid."
   Cancelled checks can serve as records of business transactions.
to subtract—the opposite of "add"; to remove, to take away one sum from another
   If you subtract 6 from 10 you get 4.
payee—the person who will receive the sum of money that a check is written for. The payee's name appears on the check after the words "pay to the order of."
   The payee must endorse his check in order to receive his money.
insufficient funds—said of a checking account balance that is too small to cover a check that the account holder has written
   If your balance is $200.00 and you write a check for $300.000, you are overdrawn. You have insufficient funds for the payment of the check.

Supplementary Vocabulary

monthly—every month
   The bank sends checking account customers a monthly statement.
hourly—every hour
daily—every day
weekly—every week
quarterly—every three months (**a quarter** = a quarter of a year)
yearly—every year (also: **annually**)
minimum—the smallest amount
maximum—the largest amount

Vocabulary Practice

Select the answer that correctly completes each sentence.

1. The bank charges a _____ to cover the cost of bookkeeping.
   a. payee   b. transaction   c. fee
2. I wrote a check for more money than I have in my account. I'm afraid I'm _____.
   a. overdrawn   b. insufficient funds   c. minimum balance
3. The monthly statement gives you a record of all the _____ of your checking account.
   a. demand deposits   b. cancelled checks   c. transactions
4. A check that can be signed over to a third party is _____.
   a. subtracted   b. negotiable   c. overdrawn
5. "You are allowed to write up to ten checks without a service charge." "That's all? You mean ten checks is the _____?"
   a. balance   b. maximum   c. minimum

CHECKING ACCOUNTS

In the United States, checking accounts are available only at commercial banks. Commercial banks specialize in demand deposits, such as checking accounts. A checking account is money that a customer deposits in order to use that money to write checks. Savings accounts pay the depositor interest but checking accounts do not. In fact, checking account customers pay the bank a service charge for the bookkeeping involved in administering the account.

The method of recordkeeping is also different in savings accounts and checking accounts. A depositor must present his passbook for any savings account transaction. The bank records these transactions in the depositor's passbook. Checking account customers, however, do not have passbooks. They themselves record the amounts of the checks that they write and they receive a monthly statement from the bank. This statement lists all the checks that the bank paid and all deposits that the account holder made during the month. The bank usually sends the statements with the customer's cancelled checks. The customer then compares the balance on the statement with the balance in his own records by subtracting the total of his outstanding checks.

There are other fees that the bank may collect from checking account holders. For instance, banks charge a fee for stopping payment on a check. When a depositor decides that he doesn't want the bank to pay a payee, but he has already written a check to that person, he may give the bank a stop payment order. The bank will then refuse to pay this check, and charges the depositor a fee. Banks also charge a depositor a fee when he is overdrawn. A depositor is overdrawn when he writes a check for more money than the balance in his account. The bank marks the check "insufficient funds," returns it, and charges a penalty for it. In everyday language we say that a check returned for insufficient funds has "bounced."

Recent changes in banking regulations have allowed savings banks to offer negotiable order of withdrawal accounts. These accounts, called N.O.W.

accounts, are very similar to checking accounts but they pay interest like savings accounts. The depositor can write withdrawal orders against the balance in the account. These withdrawal orders look like checks, and depositors receive a monthly statement summarizing deposits and withdrawals. There is often no service charge if depositors keep a minimum balance in their accounts. Commercial banks also offer N.O.W. accounts.

As far as checking accounts go, the difference between savings banks and commercial banks is growing smaller in the U.S.

Comprehension Check

A. State whether each statement is true or false based on the reading.

1. Checking accounts are available at savings banks.
2. Both checking accounts and savings accounts pay interest.
3. Checking account holders receive a monthly statement from the bank.
4. There is no fee for a stop payment order.
5. N.O.W. accounts are not available at savings banks.

B. Combine each group of words into a sentence that expresses information contained in the reading passage. You may add whatever words are necessary to make a grammatically correct sentence.

1. checking accounts/available/commercial banks
2. savings accounts/transactions/passbook
3. bank/cancelled checks/monthly
4. N.O.W. accounts/interest
5. depositor/penalty/overdrawn

C. Answer each of the following questions orally.

1. Why do checking account holders have to pay a service charge?
2. What information appears on a monthly statement?
3. What does "insufficient funds" mean?
4. How can N.O.W. account holders avoid paying a service charge?
5. In what ways has the difference between savings banks and commercial banks gotten smaller in the U.S.?

D. **Composition**. Write a short paragraph explaining the differences between:
1. a checking account and a N.O.W. account.
2. a passbook and a monthly statement.

Building Your Vocabulary

A. Select the answer that correctly completes each sentence.

1. Money in a checking account is a _____.
   a. demand deposit   b. term deposit
2. A service charge is a kind of _____.
   a. transaction   b. fee

3. A check is a written _____ of payment.
   a. statement   b. order
4. I wrote a check to John last month, but he hasn't cashed it. That check is _____.
   a. outstanding   b. cancelled
5. I don't know how much money is in my account. I must check my _____.
   a. penalty   b. balance

B. **Rewriting sentences.** Rewrite each of the following sentences replacing the underlined word or words with the correct form of one of the new words of this lesson.

1. He <u>took away</u> 30 from 60.
2. We have not yet received your <u>instructions</u> to pay.
3. A good businessman keeps a record of all his <u>deals</u>.
4. Customers should present their passbooks <u>once a year</u>.
5. This is the <u>smallest</u> balance you can have in the account.

PRESENTATION

Irregular past tense forms

come		Mrs. Allen <u>came</u> to my window.
feel		She <u>felt</u> like staying home.
get*		I <u>got</u> my paycheck yesterday.
give		He <u>gave</u> the teller his deposit slip.
go		We <u>went</u> to the bank yesterday.
keep		They <u>kept</u> their money in this bank.
leave		The tellers <u>left</u> the bank early.
say		The manager <u>said</u> I had to sign the slip.
speak		She <u>spoke</u> with the manager.
withdraw		He <u>withdrew</u> money yesterday.

*also: forget, forgot

"When did she {go / come / leave / speak}?   Did she {go / come / leave / speak} at 2:00?"

"No, she {went / came / left / spoke} at 3:00."

Checking Accounts   13

Structure Practice

A. Restate each of the following sentences in the past. The sentences form a connected story.

Model: I work here.
→ I worked here.
1. John and Mary leave their house at 2:30.
2. They go to the bank.
3. They withdraw money from their savings account.
4. The teller gives them their money.
5. They say "thank you" to her.

B. Make each of the following sentences negative. Remember to change the form of the verb from past to infinitive.

Model: I worked here.
→ I didn't work here.
1. He felt like resting all day.
2. She kept a large balance in her account.
3. I got my monthly statement yesterday.
4. They forgot their passbook again.
5. You went home early.

C. Now make each of the sentences in exercise B into a question. Remember again to change the form of the verb from past to infinitive.

Model: I worked here.
→ Did I work here?

D. You are a teller in a bank. The manager asks you if certain things happened today. Tell him in each case that the things he wants to know about happened yesterday.

Model: "Did you work hard today?"
"No, I worked hard yesterday."
1. Did Mr. Jones withdraw money today?
2. Did you speak with Mrs. Green today?
3. Did you go to lunch at 12:00 today?
4. Did you come to the bank early today?
5. Did you get your paycheck today?

Building Sentences

A. Complete each of the following sentences with the appropriate preposition.

1. You must compare your figures ____ the figures on the bank's statement.
2. I have decided ____ opening (= not to open) a new account.
3. The bank charged me a fee ____ the stop payment order.
4. Customers may write checks ____ the money on deposit in their accounts.
5. If you subtract 40 ____ 70 you get 30.

B. Select the alternative that correctly completes each sentence.
1. The bank refused _____ that check.
   a. to pay   b. paying
2. Regulations do not allow this bank _____ checking accounts.
   a. offering   b. to offer
3. He changed his mind after _____ the check.
   a. writing   b. to write
4. Banks charge a fee for _____ an account.
   a. administer   b. administering
5. You must endorse the check _____ your money.
   a. for receiving   b. to receive

BANKING CONVERSATIONS

A. You are a bank customer. Explain to your friend:
1. why you opened a N.O.W. account.
2. why your check bounced.
3. what you do to balance your checking account.

B. As a bank employee, explain to one of your customers:
1. how she can stop payment on a check.
2. why he has to pay a service charge on his checking account.
3. how she can avoid paying a service charge on her N.O.W. account.

READING PLUS

Now that you have completed the lesson on checking accounts you should be able to read the following authentic advertisement for N.O.W. accounts at the Brookline Savings Bank. First, study these words and phrases.

to compound interest—to calculate interest on the basis of the original deposit plus interest previously earned
Federal Deposit Insurance Corporation, Deposit Insurance Fund of Massachusetts—government agencies that insure the deposits held by banks
cycle—a fixed period of time
personal check—a check written by an individual (that is, not a company or business check)
uncollected funds—checks deposited in an account that have not yet been paid by the bank they are drawn on
Reserve Credit—an automatic loan
faced with unexpected bills—owing money you did not think you would have to pay

Checking Accounts

purchasing power—having enough money to buy certain items
subject to collection—a check that is accepted subject to collection will be credited to your account only after your bank has received payment from the bank that the check is drawn on
to clear; clearance—the clearing of a check is its collection and final payment
business day—a day when banks and offices are open
to consult—to speak with, talk to, get advice from
to drop by—to come in, visit
prior to—before

Reprinted by permission of the Brookline Savings Bank, Brookline, Massachusetts, U.S.A. (1980).

Is there really a checking account that pays interest?

Yes!
The Brookline Savings Bank NOW Checking Account offers its customers all the convenience of a checking account with the income advantages of a savings account. Your money earns 5% annually, provided a balance of $10.00 is maintained. The interest is compounded continuously, paid monthly, and all deposits are insured in full by the Federal Deposit Insurance Corporation and the Deposit Insurance Fund of Massachusetts. A variety of check styles are offered and your cancelled checks are returned each month with your monthly statement.

What does a NOW Checking Account cost?

Your NOW Checking Account is absolutely free of service charges if you maintain a $200 minimum balance in your account at all times.
SERVICE CHARGES:
If your balance drops below $200 at any time during the statement cycle, you will be charged a $2.00 monthly maintenance fee and 15 cents for each check paid during the cycle.
PERSONAL CHECK CHARGES:
We will provide your first fifty checks free. The printing for additional checks (minimum order 200 checks) will cost you only about $3.85. You can expect delivery of your checks about two weeks after you place your order.
OTHER CHARGES:
There is a $5.00 charge for Stop Payment requests and a $7.50 charge for items returned due to insufficient funds or uncollected funds. There is also a $1.00 charge for returned checks deposited to or cashed against your account.

How can I get extra money when I need it?

If you apply and qualify, your NOW Checking Account can have a built in line of credit. It's called Reserve Credit, and it's a feature that allows you to write checks larger than your balance.
There's no charge until you use it, and we think you'll find it's a valuable service to have when you're faced with unexpected bills or when you want to have a little extra purchasing power. It's also great protection against accidentally overdrawing your NOW Checking Account.

Why a NOW Checking Account?

Why not? A NOW Checking Account works exactly like a regular checking account except it pays you 5% interest on the balance. The NOW Checking Account (NOW stands for Negotiable Order of Withdrawal) was developed in 1972 right here in Massachusetts.

Banking Situations

A. Imagine that you are an employee of the Brookline Savings Bank. Answer the following questions that customers have about N.O.W. accounts.
1. How do I apply for a N.O.W. account?
2. How much interest do I earn on my balance?
3. What is Reserve Credit?
4. How long does it take for a check drawn on a local bank to clear?
5. How much do checks cost?

B. You are a manager of the Brookline Savings Bank. Explain the following to a customer who is thinking about opening a N.O.W. account:
1. the costs of a N.O.W. account
2. what charges might arise for the customer
3. how long it takes for checks that a customer deposits to be available for withdrawal
4. how the customer can avoid the problem of uncollected funds in his account

---

How soon will checks deposited to my account be available for withdrawal?

Checks deposited to your accounts at Brookline Savings Bank are accepted subject to collection and final payment by the bank on which they are drawn. Although you begin earning interest on the day of deposit, please allow 5 business days for these items to clear through local banks and 10 business days for clearance through out-of-state banks, before you attempt to write checks on the funds.

How can I avoid the problem of uncollected funds in my NOW Checking Account?

If you are a Reserve Credit customer, we will pay checks against uncollected funds in your NOW Checking Account up to the available credit on your line.
Another way to avoid uncollected funds problems is to maintain a savings account with a collected balance sufficient to cover any check deposit you may make to your NOW Checking Account.
Should you have a question on the availability of funds on a particular deposit item, please consult a manager prior to your transaction.
Your cooperation and assistance will help us provide you with our most efficient service.

How do I apply?

To open up a NOW Checking Account, drop by any of our five Brookline offices. Or, call us and we'll mail you the necessary forms.
We would like to be of service to you.

the modern old
BROOKLINE SAVINGS BANK
changing with the times

Member FDIC/DIF

Checking Accounts

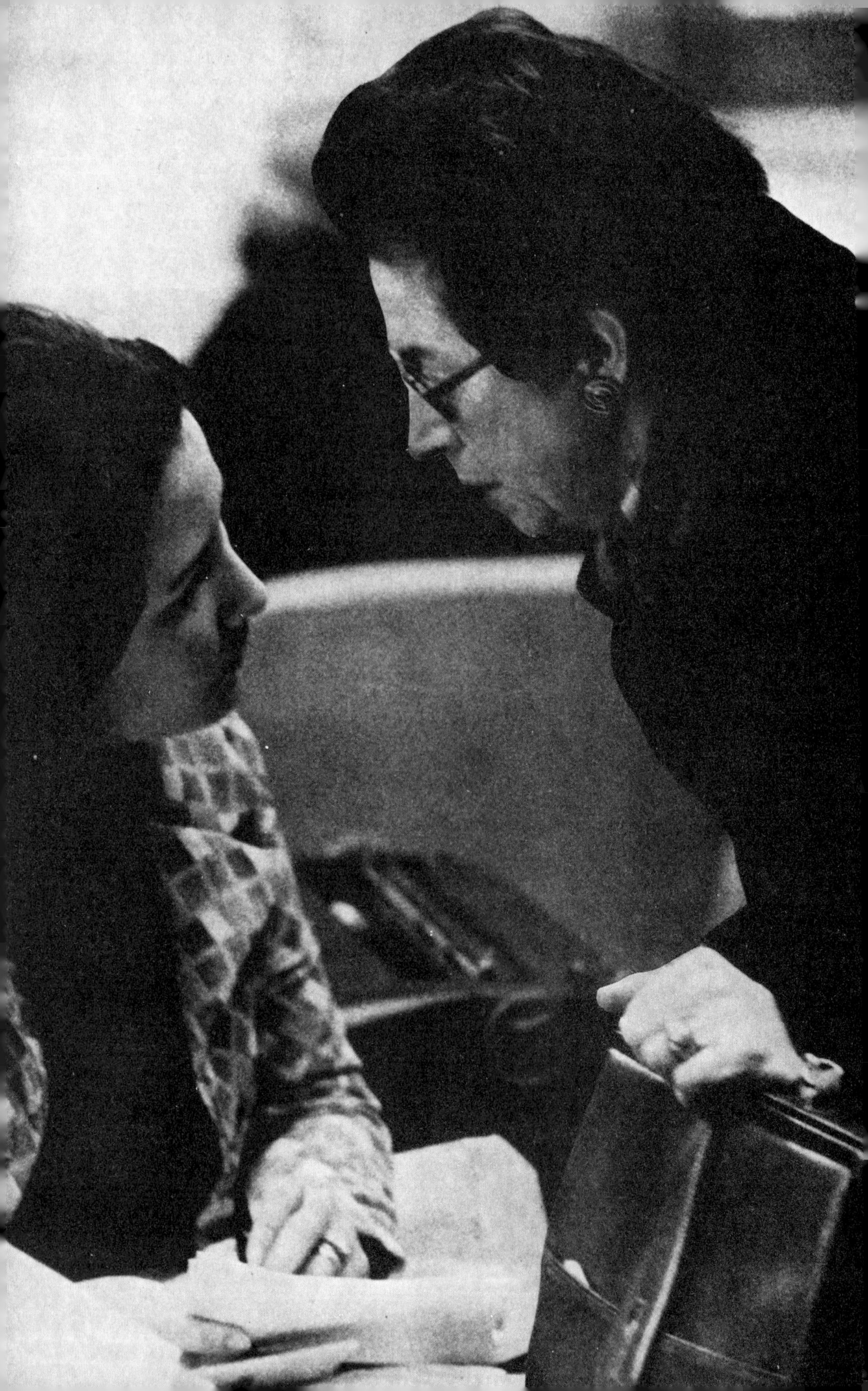

LESSON 3

LOANS

VOCABULARY

loan—money that one party gives to another to use temporarily
loan department—the section or division of a bank that takes care of loans
loan officer—officer of the bank who interviews people who want to borrow money
loan application—the form that a customer fills out when he wants a loan
currently—at the present time, at this moment
in effect—valid, currently in use
commercial loans—money that banks lend to businesses
personal loans—money that banks lend to individual borrowers
collateral—property or money that a bank takes as security for a loan
credit file—information about a bank customer who wants to borrow money
to pay back—to return the money that you borrow (also: **repay**)
charge account—an account that allows a customer to get merchandise or services immediately, but pay later
charge card—a piece of plastic with the name of the charge account holder and his charge account number. The account holder presents this card when he uses his charge account to buy something.

Expansion

to borrow—to take money from someone and promise to return it
to lend—to permit someone to use your money temporarily with the understanding that she has to return it
  I need to borrow some money. Can you lend me $100.00?
  The party who lends the money is the **lender**. The party who borrows the money is the **borrower**.
term—period of time
  The term of the loan is three years.
principal—the amount of money that the lender lends to the borrower
due—payable at a particular time
  Payments are due on the first of every month.
to default—not to pay money that is due

to take possession of—to become the owner of, to take property from another person
   If you default on your car loan the bank will take possession of your car.
to pay off—to finish paying back
debt—money that you owe
   Before you borrow any more money, you should pay off your debts.
to compute—to figure, to calculate
   The bank computes interest payments on the principal.
tenure—the term of the loan
   Long-term loans may have a tenure of ten years.
credit rating—the amount, type and term of loans that the credit department of a bank decides that it can offer a customer
creditor—lender
debtor—borrower, someone who has debts

Vocabulary Practice

Select the answer that correctly completes each sentence.

1. If you need money I can _____ you some.
   a. pay back   b. borrow   c. lend
2. When my friend needed a loan he offered the bank his house as _____.
   a. debt   b. term   c. collateral
3. James has not paid back two loans. He must have a terrible _____.
   a. credit rating   b. charge card   c. principal
4. If you _____ your car loan, the bank will take possession of your car.
   a. pay off   b. default on   c. compute
5. In order to calculate the monthly payments on your loan, the bank adds the interest to the _____ and divides the total by the number of months.
   a. tenure   b. principal   c. charge account

AN AUTO LOAN

John Baker works in the loan department of a bank in Denver, Colorado. He is a loan officer. Stanley Fanelli has an appointment with him now to ask about a loan. He needs money to buy a new car.

Mr. B.   Hello, Mr. Fanelli. Please have a seat. What can I do for you today?
Mr. F.   I want to borrow some money to buy a car. A friend of mine, Jack Richardson, bought a new car last week. He told me that he got his loan here.
Mr. B.   Oh yes. I remember him. I was the loan officer who spoke with him.
Mr. F.   He said that you were very helpful. I know very little about loans and I hope you can explain things to me.
Mr. B.   I will certainly try. What questions did you have for me?
Mr. F.   First, I want to know if loans for buying cars are commercial loans or personal loans.
Mr. B.   Neither, Mr. Fanelli. They're auto loans. A commercial loan is principal that banks lend to businesses. Personal loans are made to individuals, but not for buying cars.
Mr. F.   What about interest rates?
Mr. B.   The rate of interest currently in effect on auto loans is 16%.
Mr. F.   For how long will I have to make monthly payments?
Mr. B.   The term of the loan is three years, so there will be 36 monthly payments.
Mr. F.   Do I have to give the bank any collateral?
Mr. B.   The car serves as collateral. If you default, the bank can take possession of the car. The bank also checks your credit file to make sure that you always paid back your loans in the past. Do you have any charge accounts?
Mr. F.   My wife and I bought our furniture with our charge card and we even used it to buy airplane tickets for our vacation in California last year. We paid off both those debts promptly.
Mr. B.   That's very good. I assume there will be no problem. But the first thing you have to do is fill out this loan application.
Mr. F.   Thank you very much. I'll start right now.

Comprehension Check

A. State whether each statement is true or false based on the dialogue between John Baker and Stanley Fanelli.

   1. Mr. Fanelli needs a loan to buy his new car.
   2. A teller gave him the loan.
   3. Car loans are personal loans.
   4. The tenure of auto loans is three years.
   5. Mr. Fanelli doesn't have any charge accounts.

B. Answer the following questions orally.

1. Which part of the bank takes care of loans?
2. What do you have to fill out if you want a loan?
3. How did Mr. Fanelli learn about loans?
4. What kind of loan is a commercial loan?
5. Will Mr. Fanelli make monthly payments?
6. What is the current rate of interest on car loans?
7. How does Mr. Fanelli's new car serve as collateral for the loan?
8. How does the bank decide whether or not to give Mr. Fanelli a loan to buy a new car?
9. What did Mr. Fanelli and his wife use their charge card for?
10. Did Mr. Fanelli and his wife pay off their debts in the past?

C. Composition. Write a short paragraph explaining what a bank customer has to do in order to get an auto loan.

Building Your Vocabulary

A. Find the words in the right-hand column that match in meaning the words in the left-hand column.

1. in effect
2. pay back
3. security
4. calculate
5. term
6. at present
7. business loan
8. borrower
9. money you owe
10. not pay off

a. commercial loan
b. collateral
c. debtor
d. valid
e. currently
f. tenure
g. repay
h. compute
i. default
j. debt

B. Make each pair of sentences have the same meaning by completing the second sentence of each pair with the proper form of one of the new words of this lesson.

Model: She took out a loan for $10,000.
         The _____ of her loan was $10,000. Answer: principal

1. The bank checks information about borrowers.
   The bank checks borrowers' _____.
2. I can buy things at the store with my charge card.
   I have a _____ at that store.
3. At last I don't owe the bank any more money.
   I've _____ my loan.

22

4. He owes money to a lot of people.
   He has a lot of _____.
5. I have to pay back the loan in six months.
   The bank gave me a short-_____ loan.

PRESENTATION

I. More irregular past tense forms

buy	bought	Stanley Fanelli <u>bought</u> a new car.
know	knew	Stanley <u>knew</u> very little about loans.
lend	lent	The bank <u>lent</u> Stanley money.
make	made	John Baker <u>made</u> a lot of money last year.
mean	meant	He <u>meant</u> he applied for a loan.
pay	paid	They <u>paid</u> off their debts promptly.
see	saw	I <u>saw</u> the manager of the bank.
take	took	The bank <u>took</u> possession of his car.
tell	told	The employee <u>told</u> me the current rate of interest.
think	thought	I <u>thought</u> it was difficult to get a loan.

II. Combining sentences: sentences with two clauses

I know something. He works in a bank.

→ I know (that) he works in a bank.

He sees something. They have a new car.

→ He sees (that) they have a new car.

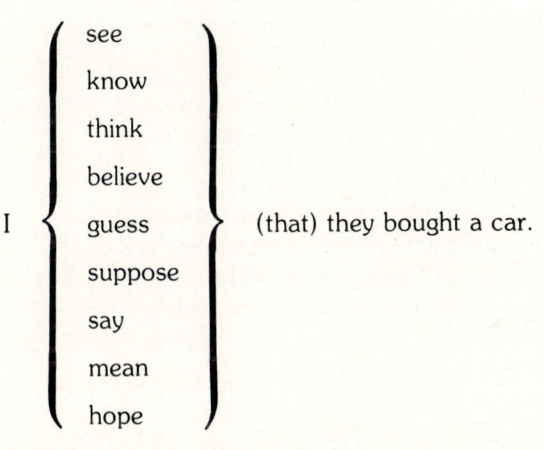

I { see, know, think, believe, guess, suppose, say, mean, hope } (that) they bought a car.

Structure Practice

A. Restate each of the following sentences in the past. Then make each sentence negative.

Model: I see Bill. → I saw Bill.
→ I didn't see Bill.

1. Bill buys a new car.
2. The bank lends him the money.
3. He tells me about it.
4. He makes a payment every month.
5. He pays off the loan in four years.

B. Combine each pair of sentences into one.

Model: The loan department is closed. I know it.
→ I know the loan department is closed.

1. Interest rates are high. We believe it.
2. Al defaulted on his loan. Mary said that.
3. The Browns are not in debt. Everyone supposes so.
4. You have filled out your loan application. I see that.
5. You have enough information. Do you mean that?

C. Rewrite each question and answer as a single sentence having two clauses.

Model: "Does Nancy have a new car?"
"Bill says so."
→ Bill says (that) Nancy has a new car.

1. "Are interest rates high for car loans?"
 "I guess so."
2. "Do George and Ellen have a good credit rating?"
 "The bank thinks so."
3. "Do they need a loan?"
 "I suppose so."
4. "Is it easy to open a charge account?"
 "We hope so."
5. "Does the bank ask for collateral for commercial loans?"
 "They know so."

D. Use each string of elements to write a two-clause sentence based on the lesson dialogue. Add any necessary words.

Model: Bill/see/Stanley/buy/new car
→ Bill sees that Stanley buys a new car.

1. Stanley Fanelli/say/bank/lend him/money
2. Stanley/think/be complicated/to get a loan
3. John Baker/explain/be easy/to get a loan
4. bank/know/Stanley/always/pay back/debts
5. John Baker/suppose/Stanley/have/charge accounts

Building Sentences

A. Complete each sentence by adding the appropriate preposition.

1. What is the interest rate now _____ effect?
2. Banks lend money _____ businesses and private individuals.
3. You can get a personal loan _____ 15% interest.
4. He's thinking _____ buying a new car.
5. Did you pay for the hotel room _____ your charge card?

B. Select the form of the verb that correctly completes each of the following sentences.

1. Do you mind my _____?
   a. ask   b. asking
2. I have to _____ some money.
   a. borrowing   b. borrow
3. Can you _____ me any?
   a. lending   b. lend
4. She told me about _____ in the bank.
   a. waiting   b. wait
5. I asked the teller _____ things.
   a. to explain   b. for explaining

C. Restate each short sentence by moving the underlined noun to a position before the preceding noun. The sentences form a connected story.

Model: She works in a bank for <u>savings</u>.
    → She works in a savings bank.

1. I wanted a loan for a <u>car</u>.
2. I filled out an application for the <u>loan</u>.
3. I asked about the rates of <u>interest</u>.
4. The bank checked the file on my <u>credit</u>.
5. They gave me a loan for <u>three years</u>.

BANKING CONVERSATIONS

1. Explain to a customer what she has to do to get a loan to buy a car.
2. Discuss some of the different kinds of loans that are available at your bank.

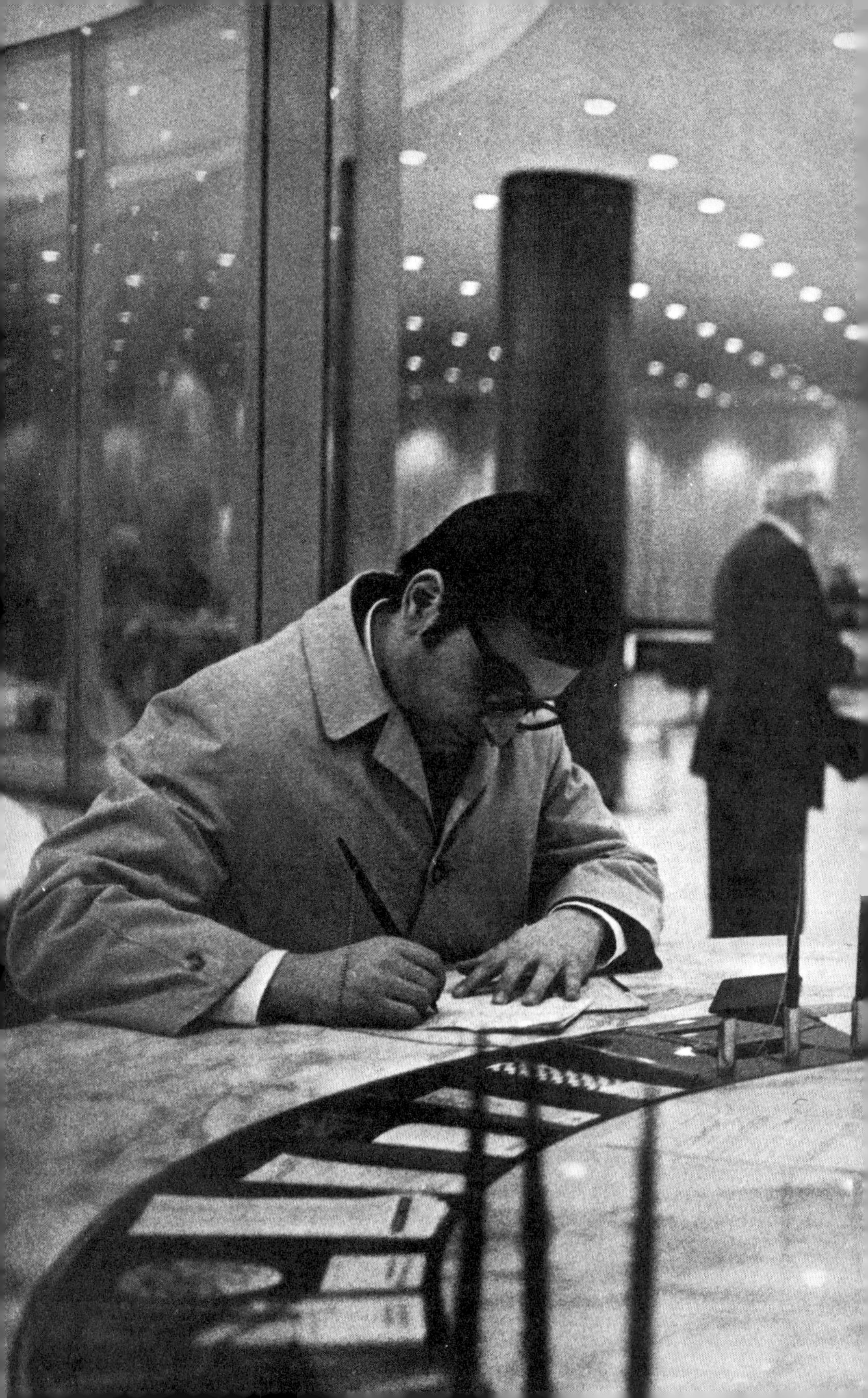

LESSON 4

MORTGAGES

VOCABULARY

mortgage—a written document that transfers (moves) ownership of property
   Mortgages are used in the purchase of houses or land.
real estate, real property—immovable property, such as land or buildings
mortgage loan—money that a lender, usually a bank, lends to someone for the purchase of real property
mortgage department—division of a bank that is in charge of mortgages
instrument—a written document, such as a deed or contract
conveyance—a document that transfers (moves) ownership of property from one party to another, such as from a seller to a buyer
   A mortgage is an instrument of conveyance.
title—evidence or proof of ownership
mortgagee—a lender of money used to buy real estate
mortgagor—a borrower of money used to buy real estate
to finance—to find or supply money for something
money supply—the amount of money available for use
tight—not easy to find, difficult to get (said of money)
fixed—cannot be moved, stable
to vary—to change, become different
variable—changeable, changing
to foreclose the mortgage—to take possession of real property if the mortgagor defaults in his payments
to guarantee—to assure, promise
guaranteed-rate period—a length of time during which the lender or the borrower cannot change the interest rate
certificate of deposit—a term-deposit account
purchase price—the actual cost of the real property

Expansion

certificate—a document declaring a fact, qualification, or promise
risk—possibility of loss; chances of a borrower defaulting
   Alan and his wife Susan are good risks. It's easy for them to get loans.

life—duration, period a contract is in effect
 In fixed-rate mortgages the rate of interest the bank charges remains the same during the life of the mortgage.
to adjust—to change; to make something fit, to change something to make it correspond to something else
 The bank adjusts its mortgage rates to the rates of interest it pays on deposits.
limit—end, border, highest or lowest amount
 There is no limit on the rate of interest they may charge.
to fluctuate—to change or vary constantly, to be continually rising or falling
 When the economy is unstable, prices fluctuate.
down payment—the portion of the purchase price that the buyer pays
 Bill and Judy want to buy a house that costs $100,000. They will make a 20% down payment and get a mortgage loan for the remaining $80,000.

Vocabulary Practice

Select the response that correctly completes each sentence.

1. A mortgage is a type of _____.
   a. supply   b. conveyance   c. limit
2. He wants to get a loan to _____ some improvements in his factory.
   a. fluctuate   b. adjust   c. finance
3. Interest rates are high because money is _____.
   a. guaranteed   b. variable   c. tight
4. They'll never get a mortgage; they're bad _____.
   a. risks   b. mortgagees   c. financers
5. There will be no change in the interest rate during the _____ of the mortgage.
   a. life   b. limit   c. title

WORD STUDY

rise — rose — risen
raise — raised
fall — fell — fallen
lower — lowered

---

to rise—to go up
to fall—to come down
    Today interest rates rose one percent.
    Yesterday interest rates fell two percent.
to raise—to make or cause something to go up
to lower—to make or cause something to come down
    The bank plans to raise the rate of interest it pays on savings accounts.
    I want to buy a house next year. I hope the banks will lower the rates on mortgage loans.

Practice

A. Complete each sentence by selecting the correct form of *raise* or *rise*.

1. People are buying less these days because prices are _____.
   a. rising   b. raising
2. My boss _____ my salary.
   a. rose   b. raised
3. The cost of living has _____ three percent.
   a. risen   b. raised
4. Fees for a stop payment order will _____ next month.
   a. rise   b. raise
5. My bank plans to _____ the minimum balance for N.O.W. accounts.
   a. rise   b. raise

B. Complete each sentence by adding the correct form of *fall* or *lower*.

1. Last week they _____ the rates on certificates of deposit.
   a. lowered   b. fell
2. Last year at this time interest rates were _____.
   a. lowering   b. falling
3. The number of depositors at that bank has _____ considerably.
   a. lowered   b. fallen
4. My bank has just _____ its rates for mortgage loans.
   a. lowered   b. fallen
5. This storekeeper plans to _____ all his prices.
   a. lower   b. fall

APPLYING FOR A MORTGAGE

Susan Thomas and her husband Alan have decided to buy a house. They have seen one that they like and now have to get a mortgage loan. Susan goes to see Joan Bentley. Ms. Bentley works in the mortgage department of the Yorktown Bank in Texas, where the Thomases live.

Ms. B.   Hello, Mrs. Thomas. How are you today? I hear you want to apply for a mortgage loan with us.

Mrs. T.   That's right. I hope you have the time to answer some questions, though. My husband and I have never owned any real estate before and we have only elementary ideas about mortgages.

Ms. B.   I'll be happy to help you in any way I can. What would you like to ask?

Mrs. T.   First, is there any difference between a mortgage and a mortgage loan? I have heard both terms used.

Ms. B.   Yes there is, although in everyday speech people call the mortgage loan a mortgage. The mortgage is actually a written document. In legal terms it is called an instrument of conveyance because it transfers title of property from one party to another. The mortgage loan is, of course, the money that the mortgagee lends to the mortgagor so that the mortgagor can buy a house or some other piece of real property.

Mrs. T.   I see. That's clear to me now. But something has been worrying me. Many of my friends have told Alan and me that it won't be easy to get a mortgage. I don't know what they mean—Alan and I have always held good jobs. It seems that two good risks like us wouldn't have much difficulty in getting financing for a new home.

Ms. B.   The problem isn't the element of risk. The supply of mortgage money has become very tight lately. Also, with interest rates rising, banks don't want to lend a large sum of money for 25 or 30 years at a fixed rate.

Mrs. T.   When you mention fixed rates you remind me that I have been hearing a lot about variable-rate mortgages. I'm not quite sure that I understand exactly what they are, but people say more and more banks are using them now.

Ms. B.   I can explain them to you. In the past, the borrower or mortgagor paid the same rate of interest over the life of the mortgage. Monthly payments to the bank were the same for 30 years. But with variable-rate mortgages they can be adjusted every six months to changes in the interest rates banks pay on deposits.

Mrs. T.   That sounds very upsetting to me. What if the borrower gets a very large increase? How would he meet his payments? Variable-rate mortgages must greatly increase the possibility of the bank's foreclosing.

Ms. B.   Not really. The bank can't adjust the rate more than 1/4 of one percent for any six-month period. And most banks give an initial guaranteed-rate period of six months to five years. During this period, no

Mrs. T.   adjustments are allowed. However, there's no limit to how much the rate that you pay can rise or fall over the life of the mortgage.

Mrs. T.   Why have banks begun to insist on variable-rate mortgages? The old system seemed so much simpler.

Ms. B.   I'll admit it was simpler, but changes in conditions have made it difficult for banks to keep the system of fixed-rate mortgages. With certificates of deposit and other term-deposit accounts, banks now pay very high interest rates to depositors in order to attract their money. These interest rates fluctuate, too, so banks want the protection of variable-rate mortgages.

Mrs. T.   Your explanation makes me feel more secure about variable-rate mortgages. How much does your bank expect as a down payment?

Ms. B.   Between 10 and 20% of the purchase price. Is that possible for you and your husband?

Mrs. T.   Yes. We have saved enough money for that. I would like to fill out an application.

Ms. B.   Fine. Here's one. We will be able to let you know whether we approve it or not in a week or ten days.

Mrs. T.   Thank you very much.

Comprehension Check

A. State whether each sentence is true or false based on the dialogue of this lesson.

1. Susan Thomas can't get a mortgage because she and Alan are bad risks.
2. In the past, mortgage rates were fixed for the life of the mortgage.
3. With a variable-rate mortgage, the bank can raise the interest rate on the mortgage loan 2% per year.
4. The interest rate on a variable-rate mortgage fluctuates with changes in the interest rate the bank pays its depositors.
5. The interest rate on a variable-rate mortgage can only rise—it cannot fall.

B. Answer the following questions orally.

1. What kind of a loan does Susan Thomas want to get?
2. Why hasn't it been easy to get one?
3. Why don't banks want to offer fixed-rate mortgages anymore?
4. How long is the usual life of a mortgage?
5. What is it that changes in a variable-rate mortgage?
6. How often does the bank adjust the interest rate on a variable-rate mortgage?
7. Why does Mrs. Thomas find variable-rate mortgages upsetting?
8. What is the guaranteed-rate period?
9. How much does the bank require as a down payment?
10. How long does it take for the Yorktown Bank to approve an application for a mortgage loan?

C. **Composition**
1. Write a paragraph that explains the difference between fixed-rate and variable-rate mortgages.
2. Write a paragraph about the most common type of mortgages in your country. Discuss down payments, life of the mortgage, types of rates, etc.

Building Your Vocabulary

A. **Matching.** Find the words in the right-hand column that match in meaning the words in the left-hand column.

1. proof of ownership		a. rise
2. change		b. adjust
3. amount		c. guarantee
4. assure		d. fluctuate
5. increase		e. limit
6. take possession		f. fixed
7. end		g. mortgagee
8. make correspond		h. supply
9. stable		i. foreclose
10. lender		j. title

B. **Rewriting sentences.** Rewrite each of the following sentences replacing the underlined words with the correct form of one of the new words of this lesson.
1. Mr. Adams owns a lot of land and buildings.
2. Interest rates are going up.
3. I hope this bank will supply money for my house.
4. I wouldn't lend him any money; there's too great a possibility he won't pay it back.
5. The interest rate can't change for the life of the mortgage.

PRESENTATION

I. Present perfect

I, You, We, They have cashed / deposited / endorsed / signed a check today.

He, She has cashed / deposited / endorsed / signed a check today.

Have { I / you / we / they } { cashed / deposited / endorsed / signed } a check today?

Has { he / she }

{ I / You / We / They } haven't { cashed / deposited / endorsed / signed } a check today.

{ He / She } hasn't

In the above sentences, the verb forms *cashed*, *deposited*, *endorsed*, and *signed* are past participles.

II. Formation of the past participles

   a. regular verbs
      cash + ed → cashed
      deposit + ed → deposited
      sign + ed → signed

      endorse + d → endorsed
      foreclose + d → foreclosed
      serve + d → served

   b. two-form verbs: past tense form = past participle
   John *left* early yesterday. (*left* = past tense form)
   John has *left* early again today. (*left* = past participle)

bring	— brought	— brought		lose	— lost	— lost
buy	— bought	— bought		make	— made	— made
feel	— felt	— felt		mean	— meant	— meant
have	— had	— had		pay	— paid	— paid
hear	— heard	— heard		say	— said	— said
hold	— held	— held		send	— sent	— sent
keep	— kept	— kept		tell	— told	— told
leave	— left	— left		think	— thought	— thought
lend	— lent	— lent				

Mortgages

c. **three-form verbs:** past tense form ≠ past participle
He *wrote* a check yesterday. (*wrote* = past tense form)
He hasn't *written* any checks today. (*written* = past participle)

be	—was/were	—been	give	—gave	—given
become	—became	—become	go	—went	—gone
begin	—began	—begun	know	—knew	—known
come	—came	—come	rise	—rose	—risen
fall	—fell	—fallen	see	—saw	—seen
get	—got	—gotten	speak	—spoke	—spoken
(In Great Britain: get-got-got)			take	—took	—taken
			write	—wrote	—written

Structure Practice

A. Rewrite the following story in the present perfect.

Model: I'm going to the bank.
→ I've gone to the bank.
  1. Sam is making a deposit.
  2. He is filling out a deposit slip.
  3. He is bringing the slip and his money to the teller.
  4. The teller is taking the deposit from Sam.
  5. The teller is saying "thank you."

B. Rewrite the following paragraph in the present perfect.

  1. Tom and Alice buy a car.
  2. They get an auto loan.
  3. The bank gives them the loan at 16%.
  4. Interest rates rise a lot.
  5. They tell me the loan is for three years.

C. Select the form of the verb that correctly completes each sentence.
  1. The price of gasoline is _____ steadily.
     a. rise   b. risen   c. rising
  2. My bank has not yet _____ to offer variable-rate mortgages.
     a. begin   b. began   c. begun
  3. Hasn't she _____ with the people in the loan department yet?
     a. spoken   b. spoke   c. speaks
  4. Since he defaulted on his mortgage payments, the bank _____ possession of his house.
     a. take   b. taken   c. took
  5. Does he _____ a good job?
     a. hold   b. holds   c. held
  6. How many checks did you _____ this month?
     a. write   b. wrote   c. written

7. We've _____ about variable-rate mortgages for a long time.
   a. known   b. know   c. knew
8. They say that interest rates are _____.
   a. fallen   b. falling   c. fall

Building Sentences

A. Complete each of the following sentences with the appropriate preposition.

1. He's a teller _____ the Riverside Bank.
2. We want to get financing _____ a new house.
3. I've learned a lot _____ mortgages.
4. They paid the same rate _____ thirty years.
5. The bank insists _____ variable-rate mortgages.

B. Rewrite each of the following sentences replacing *must* with *be forced to*.

1. The bank must close.
2. He must accept a variable-rate mortgage.
3. We must raise our fees.
4. I must report this to the manager.
5. They must apply for a loan at a different bank.

BANKING CONVERSATIONS

You want to get a mortgage to buy an apartment. You go to your local bank and see someone in the mortgage department. Try to convince the banker that you are a good risk. Give him or her whatever information is necessary in order to persuade him or her to approve your application.

READING PLUS

The following reading selection is taken from an actual brochure about mortgages from the Brookline Savings Bank. Before reading the passage, study the following short list of words. Then answer the questions that follow the reading.

flexible—can change or vary
to monitor—to check, verify
index—guide
rounded—raised or lowered to a number
equitable—fair, just
to regulate—to control, check
option—choice
to review—to examine, study again
notification—notice, letter of information
modestly—(here) by a small amount
annual—yearly

What is a Variable Rate Mortgage?

The Variable Rate Mortgage (VRM) is a form of home financing which uses a flexible interest rate that increases or decreases as it seeks the level of a carefully monitored index. The index used by the Brookline Savings Bank is the Federal Home Loan Bank Board's "Conventional Home Mortgage Closing Rates, All Lenders/All Homes (U.S. Effective Rate)" as most recently published in the FHLBB First District Facts, rounded to the nearest ¼ of 1%. The FHLBB rate is specifically recommended as the basis for an index by the Massachusetts Commissioner of Banks.

Because the cost of money a savings bank lends to you changes with the rate of interest it pays its depositors, the VRM is an equitable method of financing for both home buyers and lenders. VRMs help to assure a continuous flow of money to home financing, by better enabling the bank to pay a competitive interest rate to depositors for the money it lends.

How does a VRM work?

After an initial guaranteed-rate period, ranging from six months to five years, your interest rate is subject to small, carefully regulated adjustments.

If your mortgage interest rate and the index are more than ¼% apart, your mortgage rate could change. If the index is ¼% or more below your mortgage rate, your mortgage rate *must* be decreased by the bank. If the index is ¼% or more above your mortgage rate, an increase *may* be made at the option of the bank.

How often can my interest rate change?

After your initial guaranteed-rate period, your mortgage rate will be reviewed every six months. Only one rate change is permitted every six months and it cannot be for more than ¼ of 1%. There is, however, no limit to how high or low your rate can go over an extended period of time.

Will I be notified of changes in advance?

Of course. You will be mailed written notification of any rate adjustment at least 30 days before the new rate is to go into effect. This adjustment is based on the most recent publication of the index at the time of review.

Your notification will show you the new index and your current and new interest rates.

Questions

1. What index does the Brookline Savings Bank use to determine current mortgage rates?
2. What causes changes in the cost of money that a savings bank lends?
3. How long is the guaranteed-rate period?
4. By how much may the bank increase your mortgage rate?
5. Must the bank increase your mortgage rate if the FHLBB rate increases? If it decreases?

If a rate change occurs, how much will my monthly payment vary?
The change in your monthly payment varies only modestly, depending upon your current rate, the number of monthly payments, and amount remaining on the principal. The table below demonstrates how the interest rate on a loan of $50,000 made at 9% interest for 25 years might fluctuate over a five year period.

A Loan of $50,000 at 9.00% for 25 Years

Rate	FHLBB Rate	BSB Index	Interest Rate (APR)*	Principal & Interest Payment
Original Date Of Loan	9.10	9.00	9.00	$419.60
6 Months	9.00	9.00	9.00	419.60
12 Months	9.05	9.00	9.00	419.60
18 Months	9.20	9.25	9.25	427.90
24 Months	9.77	9.75	9.50	436.06
30 Months	10.39	10.50	9.75	444.06
36 Months	11.14	11.25	10.00	451.90
42 Months	11.32	11.25	10.25	462.60
48 Months	11.08	11.00	10.50	467.04
54 Months	10.77	10.75	10.75	474.31
60 Months	10.27	10.25	10.50	465.61

*Annual Percentage Rate

Is there a penalty for prepayments?
Yes, if you prepay for any reason in the first year, you will be penalized three months interest or the balance of the first year's interest, whichever is less. In the second and third year, you will be penalized three months interest for refinancing your mortgage with another institution, but not if you sell your home. After three years there is no penalty.

How do I apply?
For further information about a Variable Rate Mortgage loan, drop by any of our five Brookline offices. Or, call us and we'll mail you the necessary forms.
We would like to be of service to you.

Member FDIC/DIF

Reprinted by permission of the Brookline Savings Bank, Brookline, Massachusetts, U.S.A.

6. Is there any limit to how high your rate can go over the life of the mortgage?
7. When does the bank inform the mortgagor about changes in his or her mortgage rate?
8. Study the example of the $50,000 loan.
   a. What was the initial rate?
   b. How many increases were there over these five years?
   c. How many decreases?
   d. How much did monthy payments rise over the five years?

MANUFACTURERS HANOVER
FACTS
CHECK OUR LOW RATES
OUR LOANS HELP YOU BUY IT, BUILD IT, OR BETTER IT.
GET THE FACTS ABOUT OUR
AUTO, HOME EQUITY, OR STUDENT LOANS TODAY.

LESSON 5

CONSUMER CREDIT

VOCABULARY

credit—confidence or trust in the borrower's promise to repay a loan; (colloquially) the loan itself
consumer credit—credit that a bank gives to individual borrowers to help them buy household appliances or to finance improvements in their homes
passbook loan—a loan that a bank gives to a borrower who uses his savings account as collateral
credit bureau—an agency that gathers information about how people have repaid their loans in the past
reporting agency—(here) another name for a credit bureau
data—information
character—a person's moral qualities
capacity—ability
loan agreement—a contract between a lender and a borrower
cash flow—enough cash to meet one's obligations; the movement of money to and from a firm or individual
budget—a list of costs and expenses
profile—a budget that helps a borrower determine his capacity to repay a loan

Expansion

on time—(here) to repay a loan in parts over a period of time
  We've bought a lot of merchandise on time over the years.
creditworthy—deserving of credit
  The bank investigated Lisa Edwards and decided she is a creditworthy individual.
co-sign—to sign a loan agreement together with the borrower. The person who co-signs a loan is responsible for the debt if the borrower defaults.
  Richard asked his mother to co-sign his car loan.
co-signer—(also called a **co-maker**) a person who co-signs a loan
installment sales credit (also: **installment plan buying**)—a loan which allows a consumer to receive merchandise, usually high-priced items such as refrigerators or furniture. The consumer makes a down payment and signs a contract to repay the balance, plus interest and service charges, in equal installments over a specified period of time.

installment—the amount of money of a debt that the borrower repays at regular intervals
They repaid the loan in monthly installments over three years.
balance—the part of a debt that the borrower has not yet repaid
The manager told Mr. Robinson that he still owed a balance of $900.00 on the loan.
to extend credit—to give or grant credit
Banks are extending credit to very few customers these days.
outstanding amount—the sum or amount that the borrower still has to pay

Vocabulary Practice

Select the answer that correctly completes each sentence.
1. We're paying for the furniture we bought in monthly _____.
   a. installments   b. budgets   c. cash flow
2. The bank uses a _____ to find out how prospective borrowers repaid their past debts.
   a. profile   b. loan agreement   c. credit bureau
3. Mr. Harris's application for a loan was approved because he is _____.
   a. creditworthy   b. on time   c. capacity
4. Because the borrower defaulted on his repayment of the loan, the bank will hold the _____ responsible.
   a. reporting agency   b. co-signer   c. budget
5. Lisa and Frank Edwards developed a _____ of monthly expenses to see how much money they would have left over to make loan payments on a refrigerator.
   a. data   b. profile   c. consumer credit

A CREDITWORTHY CUSTOMER

Charles Ferguson, the head of the credit department of the Bay Federal Bank, is speaking with Lisa Edwards. Ms. Edwards wants to borrow money.

Mr. F.   Please sit down, Ms. Edwards. What can I do for you?

Ms. E.   Thank you. I would like to apply for a loan to buy some new living room furniture.

Mr. F.   Do you have a savings account or a checking account at our bank?

Ms. E.   No, I don't. Why do you ask?

Mr. F.   Well, if you have a savings account with us, we can use your savings as collateral. Passbook loans are usually easier to get.

Ms. E.   Is there another kind of loan that I'm eligible for?

Mr. F.   Depending on the information we get from your file at the credit bureau, we decide to approve or reject your application.

Ms. E.   I don't understand what you mean by my file. What sort of information are you looking for?

Mr. F.   The bank uses a reporting agency that gives us data about prospective borrowers. The computers at the agency store data about a person's background, his history of borrowing and repayment and his employment record.

Ms. E.   I didn't realize that lenders were able to get such personal information about prospective borrowers.

Mr. F.   You see, a lender has to make sure his borrowers meet certain basic qualifications.

Ms. E.   What are some of the things that you look for?

Mr. F.   We investigate the applicant's character. We find out things such as his employment record. We also want to know how long he has lived at his present address.

Ms. E.   I'm sure you also want to know about the applicant's earnings and the number of his dependents.

Mr. F.   Very definitely. We look into the applicant's capacity to repay very thoroughly.

Ms. E.   I can tell you now that I earn a very good salary as a public relations person in a large firm and I have several charge accounts in my name. My husband and I have bought things on time before and have made loan agreements, as you will see in the file.

Mr. F.   Well, you're obviously a creditworthy woman. We would probably approve your application and would not require that your husband co-sign the loan.

Ms. E.   I'm very glad to hear that. In these times of high inflation, we have some problems with cash flow. That's why I'm applying for a loan. Now I would like to know what the finance charge would be on a $3000 loan.

Mr. F.   I'll be happy to give you that information. Also, I'll tell you about our service charge and I'll figure out the annual percentage rate.

Ms. E.   Fine. I've already prepared an estimated monthly budget. That way I'll

Mr. F.   be able to see what my repayment capacity is for the loan.
Mr. F.   That's very wise of you, Ms. Edwards. We advise our potential borrowers to develop a profile of their monthly expenses in order to see how much money they have left to make loan payments. Now, if you'd kindly fill out these forms, we can begin processing your application.
Ms. E.   Thank you, Mr. Ferguson. I appreciate all your help.

Comprehension Check

A. State whether each statement is true or false, based on the information in the dialogue.

1. Lisa Edwards has a checking account at the Bay Federal Bank.
2. It is easier to get a passbook loan.
3. The credit bureau provides the bank with data about prospective borrowers.
4. The bank investigates the loan applicant's capacity to repay the loan.
5. Lisa Edwards has charge accounts only in her husband's name.
6. Mr. and Mrs. Edwards have bought merchandise on the installment plan.
7. Charles Ferguson requires that Mr. Edwards co-sign his wife's loan.
8. Although Lisa Edwards has no cash flow problems, she has to apply for a loan.
9. Mr. Ferguson is pleased that Lisa Edwards has developed a profile of monthly expenses.
10. The bank will probably extend credit to Lisa Edwards because she seems creditworthy.

B. Answer each of the following questions orally.

1. How would it help Lisa Edwards to have a savings account at the Bay Federal Bank?
2. How will the bank find out about Ms. Edwards's repayment of debts in the past?
3. Why does the head of the credit department of the bank say that Lisa Edwards's husband will not have to co-sign the loan?
4. What are some of the things that Ms. Edwards must know about the loan if the bank decides to extend her credit?
5. Why does Charles Ferguson advise potential borrowers to develop a profile of their monthly expenses?

C. Combine each group of words into a sentence that expresses information contained in the dialogue. You may add whatever words are necessary to make a grammatically correct sentence.

1. bank/data/reporting agency
2. Mr. and Mrs. Edwards/merchandise/on time
3. Lisa Edwards/salary/public relations person
4. high inflation/problems/cash flow
5. estimated monthly budget/repayment capacity/loan

D. **Composition.** Write a short paragraph explaining the ways in which a bank determines if a loan applicant is creditworthy or not.

Building Your Vocabulary

A. **Matching**. Find the words in the right-hand column that match the words closest in meaning in the left-hand column.

1. budget
2. loan agreement
3. in installments
4. credit bureau
5. co-signer
6. data
7. capacity

a. reporting agency
b. ability
c. information
d. profile
e. on time
f. contract
g. co-maker

B. **Rewriting sentences.** Rewrite each of the following sentences replacing the underlined word or words with the correct form of one of the new words of this lesson.

1. The bank decided to grant credit to Ms. Edwards.
2. The credit department is investigating the applicant's moral qualities.
3. My father was the other person who signed the loan agreement.
4. You can't ask for a new loan until you repay the unpaid part of the old loan.
5. This is the first partial payment of my loan.
6. The banks are not giving loans these days.
7. Banks grant loans using the borrower's savings accounts as collateral more easily than other types of loans.

PRESENTATION

I. Direct objects

subject	verb	direct object
My husband and I	have	several charge accounts.
We	have made	loan agreements.
The bank	would approve	your application.
You	haven't filled out	these forms.

II. Indirect objects

subject	verb	indirect object	remainder
The employee	told	me	about the service charge.
The teller	helps	you.	
The bank	advises	potential borrowers	to develop a profile.

III. Direct and indirect objects in the same sentence

subject	verb	indirect object	direct object
The reporting agency	gives	us	data.
The bank	can't give	you	that information.

subject	verb	direct object	indirect object with *to*
The credit bureau	gives	data	to the bank.
The bank	can't give	that information	to you.

IV. Direct and indirect objects in the same sentence. Direct object is a clause.

subject	verb	indirect object	direct object clause
Mrs. Edwards	told	the credit manager	that she had prepared a budget.
Charles Ferguson	showed	her	how much she would pay each month.

Structure Practice

A. Restate each of the following sentences changing the word order as in the model.

Model: They'll give *us that information*.
→ They'll give that information to us.

1. The credit bureau sends them data.
2. The Bay Federal Bank offered its customers passbook loans.
3. Ms. Carson will bring us a profile of expenses.
4. I owe the bank the next installment.
5. The credit department wrote her a letter.
6. They're going to pay him the balance.
7. John's co-signer had to pay me the money.
8. We've offered Lisa and Frank Edwards credit.
9. Did you give them the information?
10. I'll lend you the outstanding amount.

B. Organize the following strings of elements into sentences including direct object and indirect object pronouns.

Model: money/I/her/owe
→ I owe her money.

1. a loan/give/the borrower/the lender
2. us/send/data/they
3. that bank/them/credit/extend
4. write/the credit manager/me/a contract
5. you/him/furniture/buy
6. she/the balance/the bank/pay
7. you/the down payment/lend/he
8. show/the budget/Charles/me

C. Organize the following strings of elements into sentences as in the model. Use the past tense. Note: the verbs of sentences 2, 3, 5, and 7 require the preposition *to* before the indirect object.

Model: he/tell/her/he/working
→ He told her he was working.

1. we/write/the/we/paying on time
2. I/explain/him/they/investigating/his character
3. she/mention/you/she/co-signing/a loan
4. Mr. Ferguson/tell/us/he/not extending/more credit
5. the bank/say/it/calculating/annual percentage rate
6. you/inform/the secretary/you/applying/for consumer credit
7. they/admit/you/they/defaulting/on the loan
8. he/show/me/he/receiving/a lot of data

D. Add an appropriate indirect object to each of the following sentences.

Model: We paid the balance.
→ We paid them the balance.
or
→ We paid the balance to the bank. etc.

1. I lent $3,000.00.
2. You still owe money.
3. The store will give credit.
4. The credit bureau sent the data.
5. Did she show the estimated budget?
6. I taught how to calculate the annual percentage rate.
7. That company is selling expensive furniture.
8. Lisa said she offered a large down payment.
9. We're going to bring the contracts he requested.
10. She is going to pay in monthly installments.

Building Sentences

A. Select elements from columns **A, B** and **C** to make at least ten sentences. Be sure that the sentences you form make sense.

A	B	C
Lisa Edwards	extends	a monthly budget
The bank	made	consumer credit
A borrower	fills out	a loan application
Mr. Ferguson	prepared	the reporting agency
The credit department	approves	a passbook loan
	called	data
	gives	the balance
	paid	a loan agreement

B. Complete each of the following sentences by selecting *a* or *b* for each of the blank spaces.

Model: _b_ brought _a_ the down payment.
 a. you   b. he

1. ___ offered ___ a passbook loan.
   a. me   b. they
2. The necessary information? The credit bureau sent ___ ___.
   a. it   b. to us
3. Her cash flow is good; I checked ___ ___.
   a. for you   b. it
4. Should ___ write ___ a contract?
   a. you   b. her
5. ___ have to show ___ the profile.
   a. us   b. you

BANKING CONVERSATIONS

A. You are the head of the credit department of a bank. Using the new vocabulary of the lesson, explain the following terms to a prospective borrower:
1. character and capacity
2. co-sign
3. credit bureau

B. As a loan applicant, you explain to the bank's credit manager why you need a loan and how you plan to repay it. Discuss your reasons and methods and mention the following terms in your explanation:
1. cash flow
2. on time
3. profile of monthly payments

READING PLUS

Now that you have completed the lesson on consumer credit, you can read the following credit card application from the Bay Banks of Massachusetts. First, study the following words and phrases.

membership fee—amount of money a person pays as a member of a club, society, etc.
social security no.—United States Government retirement fund (no. = number). Each U.S. citizen has a social security account number.
previous address—the address of the house where the person who is applying for the credit card used to live
ext.—extension: an extra telephone connected to the same line as the main telephone
gross—total; without deductions (opposite: **net**)
alimony—money from a husband or wife to support his/her divorced spouse (spouse: husband or wife)
child support—money to support one's child after a divorce
separate maintenance—money that one spouse pays to support the other one when they live separately (apart)
credit references—information about a person's creditworthiness
failure to disclose—if you do not tell
to disqualify—to take away a right or privilege from someone

Now read and fill out the credit card application and answer the questions about it.

Consumer Credit 47

BayBanks Credit Application

BayBank | Norfolk Trust

PLEASE CHECK ONE:
☐ INDIVIDUAL APPLICATION
☐ JOINT APPLICATION

CHECK THE APPROPRIATE BOX FOR THE CREDIT SERVICES AND BANK CARDS YOU REQUEST ON THIS APPLICATION FORM. *BE SURE TO INDICATE WHETHER THIS IS AN INDIVIDUAL OR JOINT APPLICATION.*

☐ BAYBANKS VISA
☐ BAYBANKS MASTERCARD
☐ BAYBANKS RESERVE CREDIT

You must have a BayBanks Checking or NOW account to qualify for Reserve Credit.

BayBanks Checking/NOW Acct. No.

CREDIT CARD ANNUAL MEMBERSHIP FEE - $18   ANNUAL PERCENTAGE RATE   18%

FOR BANK USE ONLY

VISA ACCT. NO.   MASTERCARD ACCT. NO.

APPLICANT: COMPLETE THIS SECTION AND SIGN BELOW.

NAME (FIRST, MIDDLE INITIAL, LAST)   SOCIAL SECURITY NO.   DATE OF BIRTH
STREET ADDRESS   CITY   STATE   ZIP CODE
HOME PHONE   OWN ☐ RENT ☐   YEARS THERE   NUMBER OF DEPENDENTS   PREVIOUS ADDRESS   YEARS THERE
EMPLOYER AND EMPLOYER'S ADDRESS   YEARS THERE   EMPLOYER'S PHONE - YOUR EXT.
POSITION   GROSS SALARY PER MONTH $ PREVIOUS EMPLOYER AND ADDRESS   YEARS THERE

CO-APPLICANT: IF JOINT APPLICATION PLEASE COMPLETE THIS SECTION AND SIGN APPLICATION BELOW.

NAME (FIRST, MIDDLE INITIAL, LAST)   SOCIAL SECURITY NO.   DATE OF BIRTH
COMPLETE THIS SECTION IF DIFFERENT FROM APPLICANT ▶   STREET ADDRESS   CITY   STATE   ZIP CODE
HOME PHONE   OWN ☐ RENT ☐   YEARS THERE   NUMBER OF DEPENDENTS   PREVIOUS ADDRESS   YEARS THERE
EMPLOYER AND EMPLOYER'S ADDRESS   YEARS THERE   EMPLOYER'S PHONE - YOUR EXT.
POSITION   GROSS SALARY PER MONTH $ PREVIOUS EMPLOYER AND ADDRESS   YEARS THERE

NAME OF NEAREST RELATIVE NOT LIVING WITH YOU   RELATIONSHIP   ADDRESS   ☐ APPLICANT   ☐ CO-APPLICANT

You need not disclose income from alimony, child support or separate maintenance unless you wish such income considered in the credit determination.

OTHER INCOME - LIST SOURCES, MONTHLY AMOUNTS, RECIPIENT (APPLICANT OR CO-APPLICANT)

	BANK	ACCOUNT NUMBER	BALANCE $	THIS ACCOUNT IN NAME(S) OF: ☐ APPLICANT ☐ CO-APPLICANT
CHECKING ACCOUNT				
SAVINGS ACCOUNT				

CREDIT REFERENCES: Show all debts, including Banks, Finance Companies, Stores and Credit Cards. If none, enter paid loan credit references. Failure to disclose all debts will disqualify this application. (Add additional sheets if necessary) Be sure to sign application below.

CREDIT TYPE, CREDITOR AND ACCOUNT NUMBER (SHOW IF JOINT OR INDIVIDUAL)	ORIGINAL AMOUNT	UNPAID BALANCE	MO. PAYMENT OR RENT	THIS ACCOUNT IN NAME(S) OF:
MORTGAGE BANK OR LANDLORD NAME				☐ APPLICANT ☐ CO-APPLICANT
AUTO LOAN				☐ APPLICANT ☐ CO-APPLICANT
OTHER				☐ APPLICANT ☐ CO-APPLICANT
OTHER				☐ APPLICANT ☐ CO-APPLICANT
OTHER				☐ APPLICANT ☐ CO-APPLICANT
OTHER				☐ APPLICANT ☐ CO-APPLICANT

COMPLETE THIS INFORMATION *ONLY* IF YOU ARE APPLYING FOR RESERVE CREDIT.

I/We have read the Reserve Credit Agreement attached to this application and agree to its terms. Please attach Reserve Credit privileges to any BayBanks card(s) issued to my/our account.

CHECK HERE FOR AUTOMATIC PAYMENT ☐   I authorize the Bank to transfer the minimum monthly payment due each month on my Reserve Credit account from my checking or NOW account.   FOR BANK USE ONLY ▶

COMPLETE THIS INFORMATION *ONLY* IF YOU ARE APPLYING FOR BAYBANKS VISA OR MASTERCARD.

☐ I/We have selected a password(s) below.

Everything stated in this application is correct. You may retain this application whether or not it is approved. You are authorized to check my/our credit and employment history and to provide information to others about your credit experience with me/us. I/We agree that use of my/our account and any cards you issue will be subject to your credit agreement and other applicable rules and regulations.

SIGNATURE OF APPLICANT   DATE
SIGNATURE OF CO-APPLICANT   DATE

Reprinted by permission of the Bay Banks of Massachusetts, U.S.A. (1980).

Questions

1. How many people can apply for membership with this application?
2. Which well-known credit cards can you apply for?
3. What is the yearly cost of membership?
4. What is some of the personal data the applicant is asked to provide?
5. Why do they ask the applicant how many years he has been at his present address and how many years he was living at his previous address?
6. Why do they ask the applicant how many years he has been working at his present position and how many years he was with his previous employer?
7. Why do they ask the applicant his gross monthly salary?
8. What is some of the personal information the co-applicant must provide?
9. Why do you think they ask the applicant to name his nearest relative not living with him?
10. What other sources of income, in addition to the gross monthly salary, can the applicant or co-applicant list?
11. What information do they ask for regarding the applicant's or co-applicant's debts?
12. If the applicant or co-applicant fails to disclose all debts, what happens to his application?
13. In signing the credit card application, what do the applicant and co-applicant agree to?

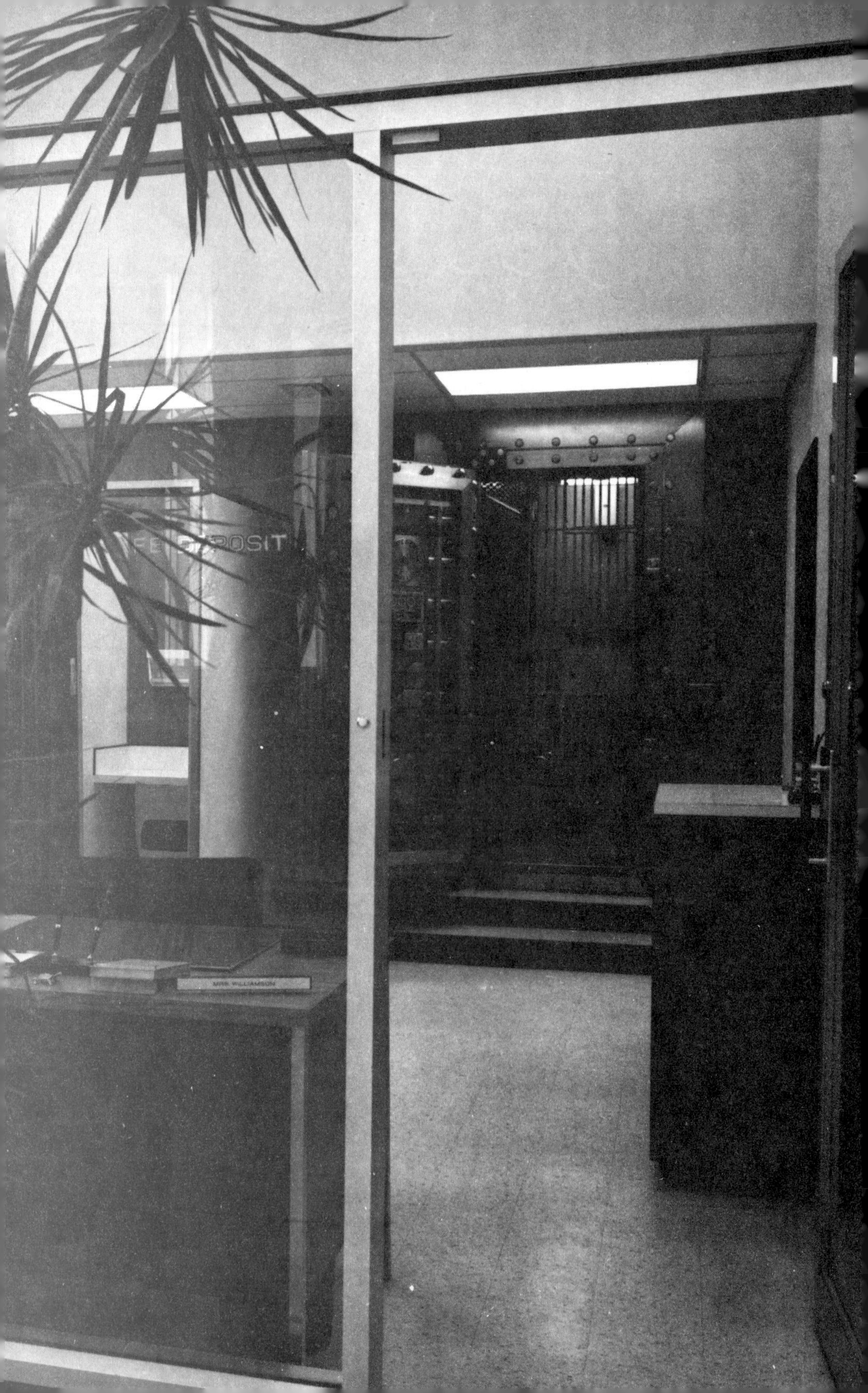

LESSON 6

WILLS AND ESTATES

VOCABULARY

will—a written document in which a person gives instructions about what to do with his property after he dies
to draw (up) a will—to write or compose a will, put a will into writing (draw-drew-drawn)
executor—person chosen to carry out the instructions left in a will
a trust—the responsibility of managing property for the benefit of someone else; also, the property held in trust
trust fund—money held in trust
trustee—a person or organization appointed to manage someone else's property
trust department—the division of a bank that takes care of the administration of trusts
estate—a person's property at the time of his or her death
to settle an estate—to pay all claims (demands for money) against an estate
estate settlement—payment of all claims against an estate
to audit—to check an account to make sure it is correct
heir—a person mentioned in a will as receiving a part of the estate
tax—a percentage of money that a person has to pay to the government
to file—to enter (a document) on public record
estate tax—taxes on an estate
a return—a written report of the taxes that a person has to pay
legacy—a gift of personal property made in a will
legatee—the party who receives the legacy
residuary legatee—the party who receives the residual legacy (the personal property that remains after the debts and taxes against the estate are paid and after all specifically mentioned legacies are distributed)
Probate Court—a court that decides whether or not a will is genuine

Expansion

intestate—without a will
to distribute—to give out, divide among two or more people
　If a man dies intestate, the state will decide how to distribute his property.

51

to name as—to choose someone for a specific function, to appoint
  He was named as our agent.
appraisal—deciding how much property is worth
  You need an appraisal of your property before you know how much tax to pay.
beneficiary—an heir, someone mentioned in a will
provision—part of a legal document that requires something specific
  There was a provision in his will that named the Church as his heir.
last will and testament—a will
to probate—to check or verify whether an instrument is really someone's last will and testament
to bequeath—to give personal property in a will
bequest—a gift of personal property made by a provision of a will; a legacy
a testator—a person who makes a will
deceased (*adj.* and *noun*)—dead person

Vocabulary Practice

Select the response that correctly completes each sentence.

1. She ____ $10,000 to charity in her will.
   a. audited   b. settled   c. bequeathed
2. You have to pay high ____ on an estate.
   a. trust funds   b. taxes   c. returns
3. The ____ will distribute the property of the deceased according to his last will and testament.
   a. heir   b. legatee   c. executor
4. In the U.S., people must fill out their tax ____ by April 15.
   a. returns   b. appraisals   c. bequests
5. My lawyer will ____ my will.
   a. draw up   b. name as   c. probate

MAKING A WILL

Jack Martin is talking with his friend, Al Henderson. It happens that Al is also Jack's lawyer. Jack brings up the subject of wills.

Jack You know, Al, I've been thinking about making a will. You probably think it's strange since I'm only thirty-five years old.

Al I don't think it's strange at all, Jack. There are many good reasons to think about a will. A will is the only way you can plan how your property will be distributed after your death. If you die intestate, then your property will be distributed according to the laws of the state. That's why I as a lawyer drew up my own will this year. I'll be happy to draw up yours for you if you'd like.

Jack Gee, Al, I didn't know you had drawn up your will. You're not much older than I am. If you don't mind my asking, who did you name as executor?

Al Well, selecting the right executor is one of the most important aspects of making a will. I decided to name the Oak Street Bank as my executor. I had already used the services of their trust department to set up trust funds for my son and daughter.

Jack So the Oak Street Bank handles estate settlement. I've been a customer there for many years. Do they have a big staff for estate settlement?

Al Very big. And the entire department serves as executor. That way there's no risk of service being interrupted.

Jack That's true. An individual executor might be sick or on vacation when you need him.

Al Exactly. And the bank is able to audit what it does as executor.

Jack How good is the bank at helping my heirs with taxes? I wouldn't want my wife and children to be faced with more tax payments than necessary.

Al The Trust Department specializes in planning for estate taxes. They'll consult with me about reporting income and expenses and they arrange for appraisals of your property. They also file estate tax returns and pay the taxes.

Jack What happens if the government has questions about the tax returns? Would my beneficiaries have to answer them?

Al No. If the returns are audited the bank will answer any questions that are raised by the government. The bank will give your heirs complete information about the taxes that are paid.

Jack What do *you* do as my lawyer?

Al Well, you give me instructions about the way in which you want your property to be distributed. You can make specific provisions about your personal property, your real estate, your savings and your other assets. You can decide about legacies to charity and you can name a residuary legatee.

Jack You've given me a lot of useful information, Al. I think we should get to work on my will right away. I'll also make an appointment with the bank's Trust Department. That way you can bring the necessary papers to Probate Court as soon as possible.

Comprehension Check

A. State whether each of the following statements is true or false based on the dialogue that you have just read.

1. Jack has died intestate.
2. The state will distribute Al's estate.
3. Naming a good executor is very important.
4. Al named the Oak Street Bank as his beneficiary.
5. The bank helps your heir plan for estate taxes.

B. Answer the following questions orally.

1. Is it strange for a 35-year-old man to think about a will?
2. What happens if someone dies intestate?
3. What does an executor do?
4. How does Al know about the services of the Oak Street Bank Trust Department?
5. Why is it a good thing that the whole staff of the Trust Department serves as executor?
6. Why does Jack want to know if the bank will help his heirs with estate taxes?
7. Who files tax returns for an estate?
8. What will your executor do if the government has questions about your tax returns?
9. What is a residual legatee?
10. Where will Al bring Jack's will?

C. Composition. Write a paragraph that summarizes the things an executor has to do after the death of a testator (the person who left a will).

Building Your Vocabulary

A. Matching. Find the words in the right-hand column that match the words closest in meaning in the left-hand column.

1. appoint
2. executor
3. without a will
4. gift
5. draw up
6. property
7. check an account
8. requirement
9. heir
10. verify

a. legacy
b. audit
c. probate
d. name
e. estate
f. trustee
g. beneficiary
h. compose
i. provision
j. intestate

B. Rewriting sentences. Rewrite each of the following sentences replacing the underlined word(s) with the correct form of one of the new words of this lesson.

1. The state will <u>divide</u> her property.
2. Mr. Ricci was <u>chosen</u> as executor.
3. His son was the principal <u>person mentioned in his will</u>.
4. He is afraid that the government will <u>check</u> his tax returns.
5. The residual legacy was small after the executor <u>paid all claims against</u> Mrs. Henderson's estate.

PRESENTATION

I. New verbs

draw — drew — drawn
choose — chose — chosen
find — found — found

II. Passive voice: be + past participle + (by + noun)

active voice: The trustees appoint him.
passive voice: He *is appointed by* the trustees.

A. Present tense

$$\left.\begin{array}{c}\text{I}\\ \text{He}\\ \text{She}\end{array}\right\} \text{is} \quad \left.\begin{array}{c}\text{We}\\ \text{You}\\ \text{They}\end{array}\right\} \text{are} \quad \Bigg\} \text{appointed} \Bigg\} \text{by the trustees.}$$

I — am
He, She — is
We, You, They — are

Note also: The trustees are appointing him.
→ He *is being appointed by* the trustees.

Wills

B. Past tense

{ I, He, She, The bank } was
{ We, You, They } were
} named as executor(s).

Note also: The teller was helping the customer.
→ The customer *was being helped by* the teller.

C. Present perfect

{ I, You, We, They } have ('ve)
{ He, She } has ('s)
} been chosen as her lawyer(s).

D. Other tenses and modals

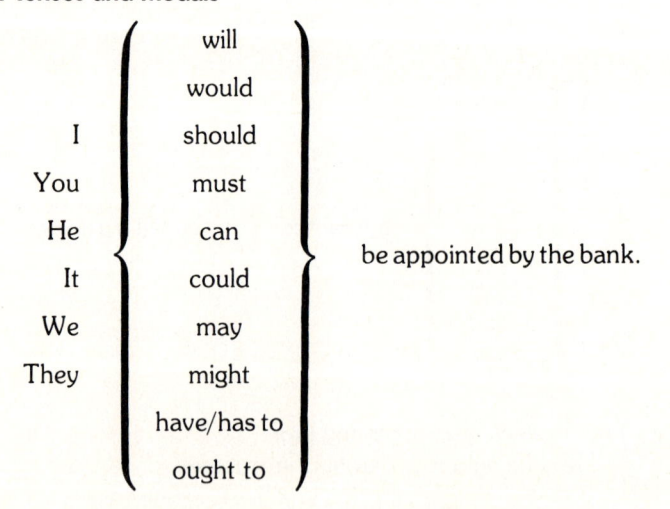

{ I, You, He, It, We, They } { will, would, should, must, can, could, may, might, have/has to, ought to } be appointed by the bank.

56

Structure Practice

A. Rewrite the following sentences about wills in the present tense of the passive voice.

Model: The manager opens the bank.
  → The bank is opened by the manager.
1. The testator chooses a lawyer.
2. The lawyer draws up the will.
3. The testator names an executor.
4. The executor carries out the instructions in the will.
5. The heirs pay the taxes on the estate.

B. Rewrite the following story about Jane's tax return in the past tense of the passive voice.

Model: Mr. Smith left $10,000 to his church.
  → $10,000 was left by Mr. Smith to his church.
1. Jane sent in her tax return.
2. The government audited Jane's tax return.
3. They found a serious mistake.
4. Jane received a letter from the government.
5. Jane had to pay an additional $1,300.

C. Express surprise that the things asked about have not yet been completed. Use a negative question in the present perfect of the passive voice.

Model: "The application must be filled out."
  "What! Hasn't it been filled out yet?"
1. The will must be drawn up.
2. His beneficiaries must be named.
3. A trust fund must be set up.
4. The estate must be settled.
5. His property must be distributed.
6. Some appraisals must be made.
7. The will must be probated.
8. Claims against the estate must be paid.
9. The returns must be audited.
10. The residual legatee must be found.

D. Using the future tense of the passive voice, tell that each of the following things will be completed tomorrow.

Model: "When will they approve the mortgage?"
  "It will be approved tomorrow."
1. When will they lower the mortgage rate?
2. When will they bring the applications?
3. When will they send out the monthly statements?
4. When will they raise the service charge?
5. When will they pay the check?

E. Change each of the following sentences from active to passive. Keep the same tense or modal in the new sentence as in the original.

Model:

The customer {endorses / endorsed / will endorse / must endorse} the check.

→ The check {is endorsed / was endorsed / will be endorsed / must be endorsed} by the customer.

1. This depositor writes ten checks every month.
2. Last week Mary Latham opened a N.O.W. account.
3. Customers must present their passbooks.
4. Both parties will sign the stop payment order.
5. The bank increased all monthly charges.
6. The bank will charge a large fee for this service.
7. Those customers didn't sign the withdrawal slips.
8. The bank doesn't record interest payments every week.
9. The bank should grant variable-rate mortgages.
10. My husband has to send our loan application to the bank.

F. Answer each of the following questions with a sentence in the passive voice. Use the elements of each cue, as in the model.

Model: "Why couldn't you give the depositor the money?"
withdrawal slip/not/sign/both parties
"The withdrawal slip was not signed by both parties."

1. When do you receive your cancelled checks?
return/bank/monthly
2. Why did that customer have to pay a service charge?
minimum balance/not maintained/in her account
3. How did you stop payment on that check?
an order/give/the manager
4. How will depositors know how much money is in their savings accounts?
all transactions/record/bank/in their passbooks
5. How do checking account holders know how much money they have in their accounts?
a record of all checks written/must/keep/them

Building Sentences

A. Link each pair of elements with the appropriate present tense form of *serve as*.

Model: Jane/head teller
→ Jane serves as head teller.
1. Trust Department/my executor
2. passbook/record of transactions
3. Mrs. Stein/trustee of the university
4. this money/down payment on the house
5. his apartment/his office

B. Expand each of the following sentences by adding the appropriate form of *to be good at*. Keep the same tense as in the original sentence.

Model: The bank helps you plan for estate taxes.
→ The bank is good at helping you plan for estate taxes.
1. The tellers help customers.
2. That lawyer drew up wills.
3. The trustees administered the university.
4. The loan department explained loans to me.
5. The executor settles the estate.

BANKING CONVERSATIONS

1. Explain to a friend why he or she should make a will. Tell your friend what has to be done in order to make a will.
2. You work in the trust department of a bank. A customer comes in who wants to know about the bank's services as executor of wills. Explain to the customer what the bank does as executor and why the bank is good at serving as executor.

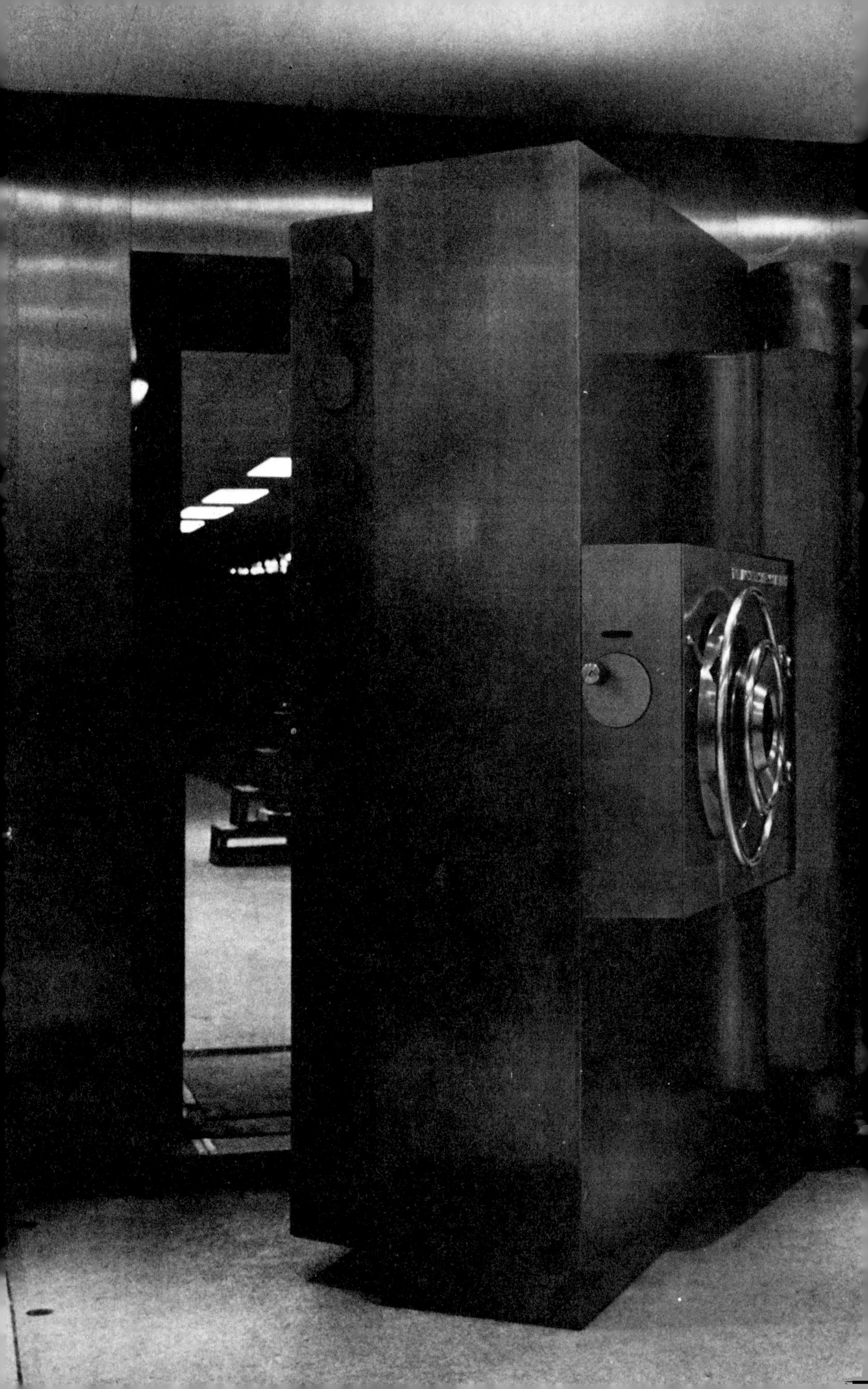

LESSON 7

THE ACCOUNTING DEPARTMENT

VOCABULARY

to enter—to record a transaction
credit—money received; in accounting, an entry made on the right side of an account
debit—money owed or paid out; in accounting, an entry made on the left side of an account
journal—book in which the records of a business are written first
ledger—record of final entry; group of accounts of a similar kind, such as the equipment ledger, accounts receivable ledger, accounts payable ledger, etc; (see Supplementary Vocabulary)
equity—the value of property left over when the liabilities against it are paid
annual report—yearly statement of financial condition
profit and loss statement—an account drawn up at the end of a fiscal period (see below)
assign—place, classify, distribute, designate
category—group, class, division
note—an instrument that is considered legal evidence of a debt
promissory notes—negotiable instruments that are written promises to pay back borrowed money to a specific creditor
commercial paper—short-term promissory notes which businesses may sell at a discount to raise cash
occupancy—cost of maintaining the building(s) where a bank is located
debentures—long-term obligations; bonds (certificates of debt)
income—earnings
expense—money spent
cash basis (also: **cash system**)—an accounting method that records transactions on the date money is actually paid or received
accrual basis (also: **accrual system**)—an accounting method that records expenses as they are made even if they have not yet been paid during the fiscal period (see below)
amortization—writing off certain expenses by dividing them into fixed payments over a period of time
lobby—main banking room of a bank where customers transact business with tellers

Expansion

accountant—person specializing in keeping or adjusting the accounts of the transactions that affect the financial health of a business
  A bookkeeper enters credits and debits; an accountant analyzes entries in an account.
fiscal period—twelve-month accounting time period
  The fiscal period of our firm is a year that ends on June 30.
premises—a piece of real estate
  Is the bank the owner of these premises?
equipment—tools, machines or other supplies needed to do a particular job
  Computers have become an important part of a bank's equipment.

Supplementary Vocabulary

accounts payable—entries of money owed to creditors
accounts receivable—money to be collected from customers

Vocabulary Practice

Select the answer that correctly completes each sentence.

1. The bank's balance sheet lists assets and _____.
   a. credit   b. liabilities   c. profits
2. Our accountant helped us figure out the _____ of the premises.
   a. amortization   b. occupancy   c. debt
3. Ms. Dijon is pleased to have a lot of _____ from her real estate holdings.
   a. equipment   b. equity   c. debentures
4. The corporation's new _____ begins on July 1.
   a. accrual basis   b. category   c. fiscal year
5. The _____ he wrote comes due in 1983.
   a. promissory note   b. statement of condition   c. ledger

A BANK ACCOUNTANT'S JOB

Jennifer Williams wants to get a job in the accounting department of a bank. She is now at an interview with Sandy Dunbar, head of the accounting department of the Twin City Bank in Minnesota. She has always worked as an accountant, but never before in a bank.

Ms. D.   Well, Miss Williams, you certainly have a lot of experience in accounting. We'd like to have someone like you work with us. The job is yours, if you want it.

Miss W.   Marvelous. I think I'll find working in a bank very challenging. But I would like some information from you. Could you specify some of the differences between an accountant's job in a bank and an accountant's job in a business firm?

Ms. D.   There are, of course, both differences and similarities. As you know, accounting has changed a lot with the arrival of computers. Bank accountants, just like company accountants, do much more than just enter credits and debits in long black journals and ledgers! One of the most important things that we do in my department is prepare the balance sheet that determines the stockholders' equity and which appears in the bank's annual report.

Miss W.   Does a bank's balance sheet look like a corporation's balance sheet?

Ms. D.   Pretty much so. It lists assets and liabilities in the same way, although some of the items are different. Oh, and at a bank the balance sheet is usually called a "statement of condition."

Miss W.   How about profit and loss statements? I've prepared a lot of those during my work as an accountant.

Ms. D.   Our accounting department prepares one at the end of each fiscal period, although I don't know if you'll be directly involved in profit and loss statements. Let me also mention that one of the most important parts of our job here is assigning entries to the proper category. In other words, accountants in a bank have to decide whether a particular entry comes under the heading of loans, notes, commercial paper, occupancy, debentures, interest income and expense, and so forth.

Miss W.   Does this bank use a cash or an accrual basis for its accounts?

Ms. D.   That depends on each item of assets and liabilities. Some are recorded on the cash system, others on the accrual system. Oh, and before I forget, another important aspect of my department's work is figuring out depreciation and amortization of premises and equipment.

Miss W.   My goodness, and to think that most people think that a bank's activity consists only of what they can see in the lobby!

Ms. D.   That's true, but most of the complex financial operations are handled in offices away from the lobby, offices that our customers rarely get to see.

Accounting

Comprehension Check

A. State whether each statement is true or false based on the reading passage.

1. The use of computers has changed the nature of accounting.
2. As an accountant, Miss Williams will merely enter credits and debits in journals and ledgers.
3. A balance sheet which appears in a bank's annual report is prepared by the tellers.
4. The statement of condition lists assets and liabilities.
5. A profit and loss statement is prepared at the end of each twelve-month period.
6. A bank accountant must determine the proper classes for entries.
7. Some of the categories that the accountant must use include notes, interest income and loans.
8. All banks use only the accrual system in their bookkeeping departments.
9. The bank's accounting department does not calculate the depreciation of premises and equipment.
10. A bank's customers and tellers transact business in the bank lobby.

B. Combine each group of words into a sentence that expresses information contained in the reading passage. You may add whatever words are necessary to form a grammatically correct sentence.

1. equity/balance sheet/determines/stockholders'
2. figures out/premises/amortization/accountant
3. accountants/debits/ledgers/entered/credits
4. statement of condition/bank's/balance sheet/is
5. headings/entries/some/debentures/commercial paper/are
6. proper/assigns/accountant/entries/category
7. recorded/liabilities/some/assets/cash basis
8. lobby/complex/not/financial/handled/operations

C. Answer each of the following questions orally.

1. What are some of the duties of a bank accountant?
2. What is a statement of condition and what does it contain?
3. How often is a profit and loss statement issued?
4. What are some of the categories bank accountants assign entries to?
5. What operations are carried out in a bank's lobby?

D. Composition. Write a paragraph describing some of the most important functions of a bank's accounting department.

Building Your Vocabulary

A. Matching. Find the words in the right-hand column that match the words closest in meaning in the left-hand column.

1. enter
2. debit
3. commercial paper
4. a piece of real estate
5. debentures
6. cost of maintaining a building
7. a bank's main room
8. record of final entry
9. classify
10. cash basis

a. assign
b. premises
c. lobby
d. occupancy
e. ledger
f. bonds
g. an accounting system
h. record a transaction
i. short-term promissory note
j. money owed

B. Rewriting sentences. Rewrite each of the following sentences replacing the underlined word or words with the correct form of one of the new words of this lesson.

1. We hired another accountant to <u>group</u> entries by category.
2. It seems that the <u>value of the property</u> of the stockholders is declining.
3. My accountant keeps the records of my business in this <u>book</u>.
4. The accountants would like to see the <u>yearly statement of financial condition</u>.
5. The bookkeeper listed <u>the money to be collected from customers</u>.
6. The <u>money spent</u> in running a business is higher every day.
7. This company is selling <u>short-term promissory notes</u> to raise cash.
8. The bank's board of directors feels it can no longer afford the expenses of <u>maintaining the building</u>.

PRESENTATION

Uncountables

They gave us { a little / a lot of } { business. / information. / money. / experience. / equipment. / support. / advice. }

I don't have much { income. / data.* / equity. / paper. / time. / work. / material. }

*For some speakers, *data* is a plural.

Accounting

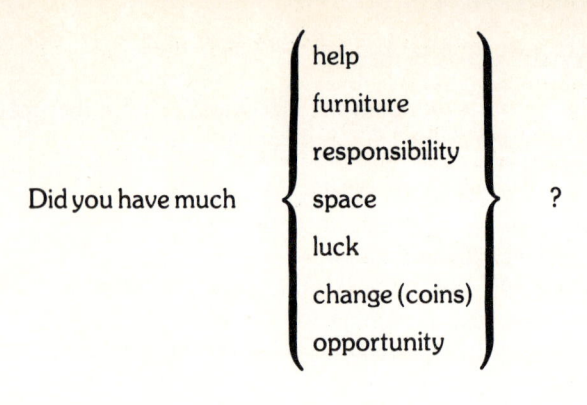

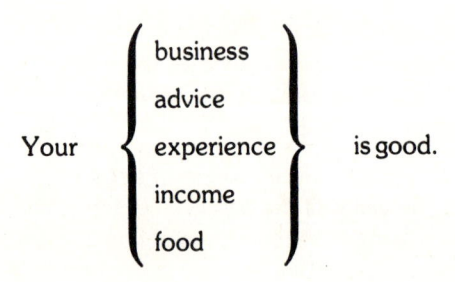

Did you have much { help / furniture / responsibility / space / luck / change (coins) / opportunity } ?

Your { business / advice / experience / income / food } is good.

Structure Practice

A. Answer each of the following questions adding *a little* before the uncountable noun.

  Model: "Has there been much concern about inflation?"
          "Not really. There has been a little concern about inflation."
  1. Is there much interest in stocks?
  2. Did you find out much information?
  3. Did they have much income from their business?
  4. Is Mr. Gordon having much luck with his loan?
  5. Is there still much work to do on the ledger?
  6. Would I have much opportunity in the company?
  7. Are the stores doing much business these days?
  8. Is there much equity in that property?
  9. Did she give you much help with the project?
  10. Were you able to get much material?

B. Answer each of the questions in exercise A adding *a lot of* before the uncountable noun.

  Model: "Has there been much concern about inflation?"
          "Yes, there has been a lot of concern about inflation."

C. Restate each of the following sentences in the negative adding *much* before the uncountable noun.

   Model: We have income from real estate.
   → We don't have much income from real estate.
   1. There's space in the lobby.
   2. Sandy has equity from her house.
   3. They bought equipment for the firm.
   4. He showed understanding for the unemployed workers.
   5. I asked them for advice.
   6. There was trouble with the computer yesterday.
   7. Our shares had value.
   8. This bank accountant has responsibility.
   9. The bank is showing support for the new accountant.
   10. You'll have to check the data.

D. Complete each of the following sentences by selecting one of the words from the list. Do not use each word more than once.

money	time	premises	company	material
space	knowledge	change	income	food
support	love	business	trading	trouble

   1. She doesn't have enough _____ to pay her bills.
   2. I have ten dollars in small _____.
   3. There's a lot of _____ in these offices.
   4. The owners have shown a real _____ of their business.
   5. The Diderots always have a lot of _____ over to their house.
   6. Mr. Lester showed little _____ for the strike.
   7. He's trying to gain some _____ about accounting.
   8. Who is the owner of these _____?
   9. You have a good _____ from your holdings in real estate.
   10. We don't have much _____ to spend at the meeting.

E. Complete each of the following sentences by adding an appropriate uncountable noun phrase.

   Model: The painting doesn't have much value, but . . .
   → The painting doesn't have much value, but it has a lot of charm, beauty, sensitivity, depth, etc.
   1. Jennifer doesn't have much ambition but . . .
   2. I don't need much money but . . .
   3. The accountant doesn't want much responsibility but . . .
   4. The tellers didn't have much data but . . .
   5. Mr. Ohno doesn't give much advice but . . .
   6. They haven't had much luck with their debentures but . . .
   7. We don't have much equity from our real estate but . . .
   8. Mr. Olsen hasn't shown much enthusiasm for the new project but . . .
   9. You won't buy much equipment for the office but . . .
   10. I haven't seen much income from the store but . . .

Accounting

Building Sentences

A. Select elements from columns **A, B, C** and **D** to form at least ten affirmative and negative sentences that contain uncountables. You may use the verbs in any tense you choose.

A	B	C	D
The bank's accountants	(no) want	much	information
We	need	any	experience
Ms. Suárez	request	a lot of	equipment
You	show	a little	money
I	have	some	responsibility
Charles	give	no	data
The accounting department	buy	lots of	interest
The premises	see	quite a lot of	business
	get	that	advice
	use	this	opportunity
	do		value
	bring		income
	send		equity

B. Complete each of the following sentences by selecting either *a* or *b*.

1. The agency will send us ____ of data.
   a. a lot   b. a little
2. Did you have ____ opportunity for advancement?
   a. no   b. much
3. There ____ much equipment in the office yet.
   a. aren't   b. isn't
4. Jennifer had ____ time to work on the ledger.
   a. little   b. few
5. How ____ their business doing these days?
   a. is   b. are
6. We haven't had ____ income this month.
   a. much   b. many
7. I have quite a lot of ____ in my pocket.
   a. changes   b. change
8. They've shown ____ interest in the ledgers.
   a. any   b. some
9. There's not ____ room in the lobby of the bank.
   a. much   b. many
10. ____ clothing is very attractive.
    a. These   b. This
11. You need ____ advice.
    a. those   b. a piece of
12. I saw ____ papers on her desk.
    a. many   b. much

C. Rearrange the elements in each of the following groups to form a sentence.

1. new/has/equipment/company/the/a lot of
2. premises/of/I/amortization/the/figure out/the
3. much/Mr. Bartlett/information/didn't/have
4. holdings/their/them/equity/give/real estate
5. on/we/business/don't/much/Mondays/do
6. experience/Sandy/a little/accounting/in/had
7. those/value/stocks/much/did/have?
8. a lot of/credits/I/time/have/and/to enter/debits
9. ask for/you/help/didn't/any
10. want/responsibility/accountant/doesn't/the/much

D. Substitution drill. Restate the original sentence using the cues in parentheses and making any necessary changes.

The bank's accountants have a lot of work.
1.   (responsibility)
2.   (a little)
3.   (want)
4.   (information)
5.   (some)
6.   (need)
7.   (equipment)
8.   (tellers)
9.   (request)
10.   (paper)
11.   (a lot of)
12.   (don't use)

BANKING CONVERSATIONS

Part of your job as head accountant in the Twin City Bank is to supervise trainees in the accounting department. As you meet with these new employees now, explain to them the function of the accounting department and what their duties are as accounting trainees.

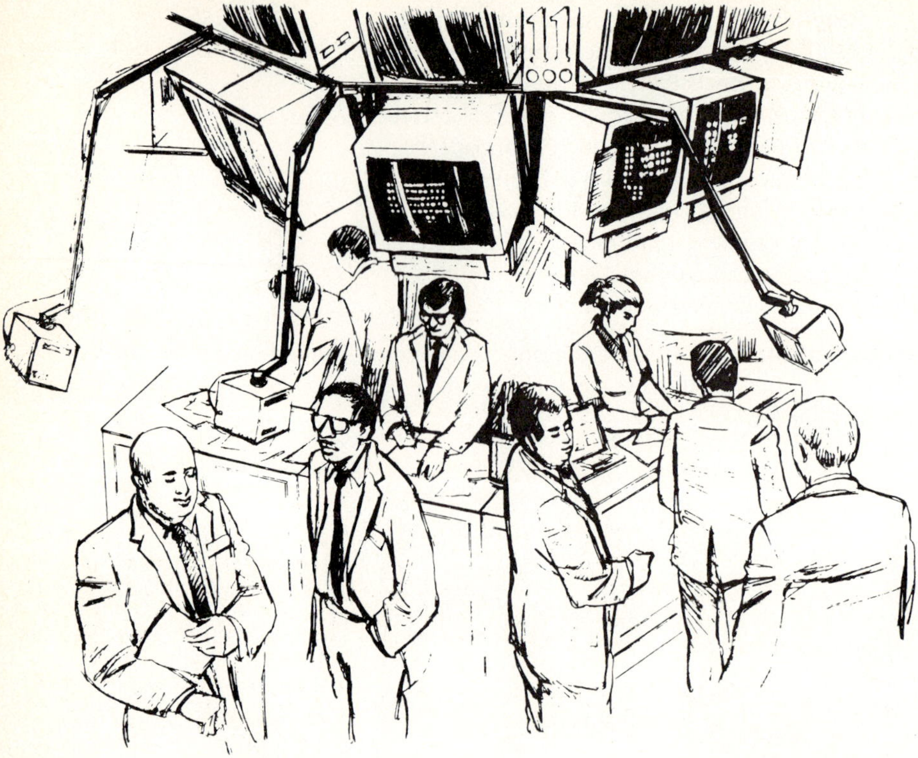

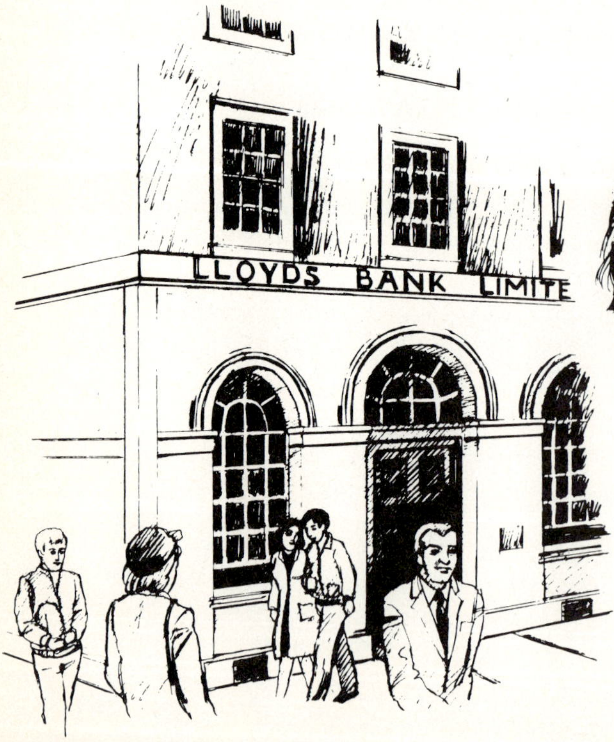
LLOYDS BANK LIMITE

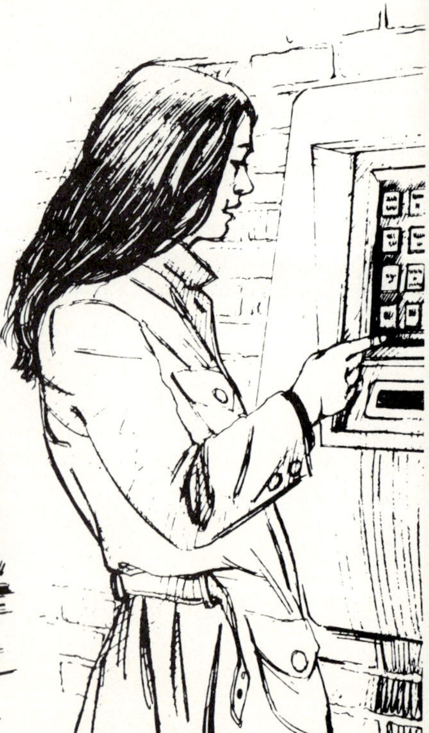

PART II
INTERNATIONAL BANKING AND FINANCE

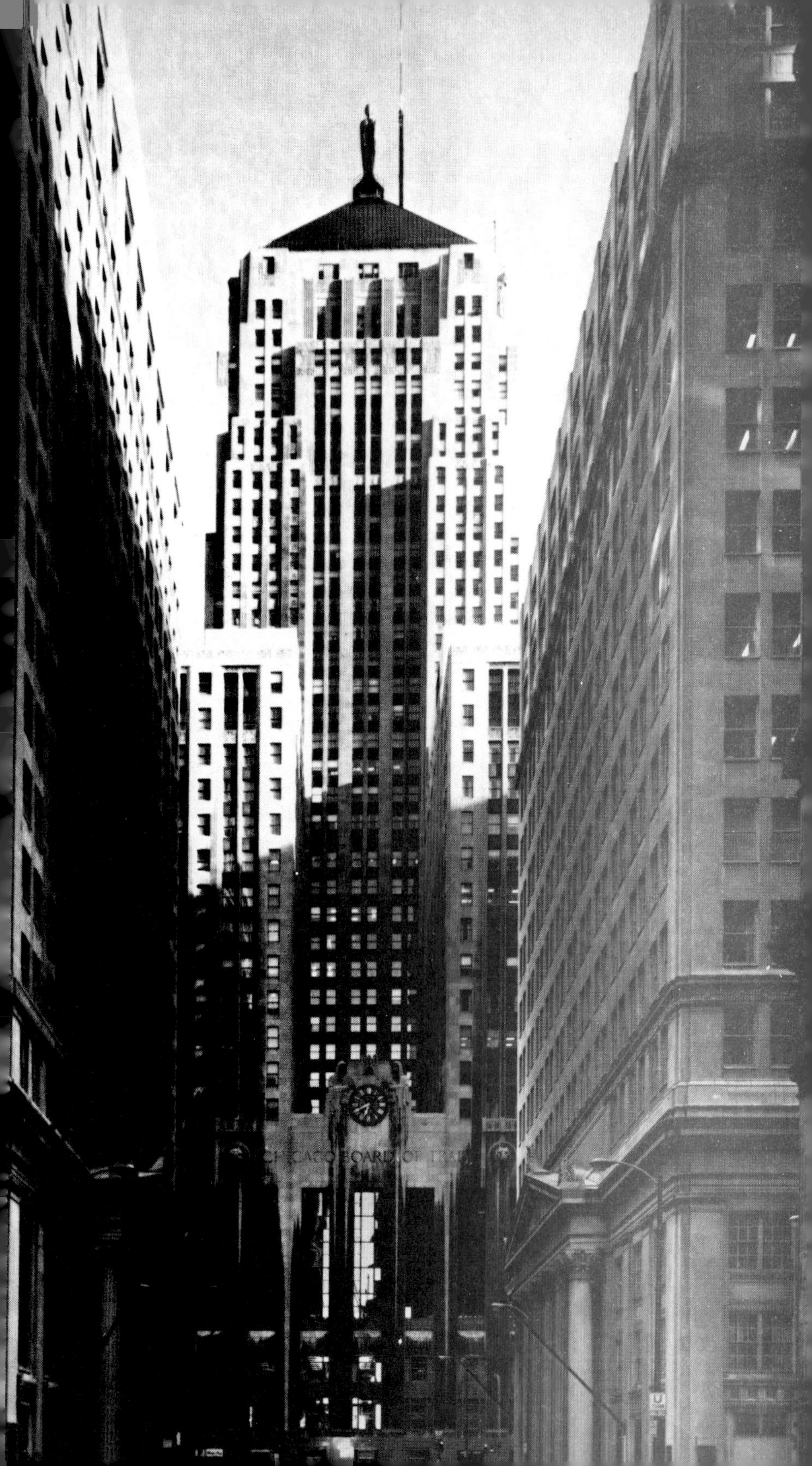
CHICAGO BOARD OF

LESSON 8

THE FEDERAL RESERVE SYSTEM

VOCABULARY

policy—a plan that determines how an organization will act in certain situations
uniform—always the same, unchanging
to set—to fix, establish
reserve requirements—percentage of total deposits that a bank keeps in cash
mandatory—obligatory, required; has to be done
ratio—proportion; a fixed relationship between two similar things
holdings—property owned; assets
advances—money paid before goods or services are received
rediscount—a negotiable instrument which has been discounted by a bank and then sold a second time to a Federal Reserve Bank and discounted again by that bank
to empower—to authorize, to give power or authority to someone
open-market—public sale of securities
security—stock or bond (see definitions, below)
to purchase—to buy; buying
investments—the money placed to purchase some kind of property with the hope of making a profit; the properties themselves that the money has been invested in
bill of exchange—an order drawn by one person on another, directing him to pay money to a third person or to his account and to charge the person who draws the order
acceptance—a bill of exchange marked "accepted"
market price—the current price
margin requirements—the percentage of the market price of securities that the buyer must pay when he borrows the money to purchase those securities
capital—money or wealth used in business
stock—a share of corporate capital
stock certificate—written evidence of ownership of stock
bond—an interest-bearing certificate of debt

Expansion

Board of Governors—a group of administrators or directors of the United States Federal Reserve System (also known as the Federal Reserve Board)
The Board of Governors sets uniform banking policies.

intervention—interference in the affairs of others; changing the normal direction of a transaction
There have been many complaints recently about government interference in the purchase and sale of securities.

volume of activity—amount of buying and selling

stock exchange—a place where stocks and bonds are regularly bought and sold
The volume of activity on the stock exchange has been very high this past week.

discount—the interest deducted from the face value of a note at the time a loan is made; the borrower receives the net amount after the discount has been deducted

Vocabulary Practice

Select the answer that correctly completes each sentence. Note: first read the passage, and then complete this exercise.

1. The Federal Reserve Board influences the volume of activity on the _____.
    a. Board of Governors   b. rediscounting rate   c. Stock Exchange
2. The Board of Governors can buy or sell United States Government _____.
    a. reserve requirements   b. securities   c. liabilities
3. _____ of the twelve Federal Reserve Banks are uniform.
    a. bonds   b. policies   c. advances
4. When margin requirements are set on the Stock Exchange, the _____ of stocks and bonds bought with loans is affected.
    a. market price   b. advances   c. open-market operations
5. Federal Reserve Banks are involved in the purchase and sale of _____.
    a. bills of exchange   b. rediscounts   c. ratios of holdings

THE FEDERAL RESERVE SYSTEM

The Federal Reserve System of the United States performs many of the functions of the Central Bank of other countries. The territory of the United States is divided into twelve Federal Reserve Districts, each one of which has a Federal Reserve Bank in a major city. Policies of these twelve banks are uniform, however, because they are set by the Board of Governors of the Federal Reserve System.

It is precisely this Federal Reserve Board that carries out operations similar to those that are the responsibility of Central Banks in Europe, Latin America and elsewhere. For instance, member banks are told by the Federal Reserve Board what current reserve requirements are, that is, the mandatory cash ratio of holdings to liabilities. Federal Reserve Banks may extend credit to member banks through advances or rediscounts. The rediscounting rate is set by each of the individual member banks. The Board is also empowered to conduct certain open-market operations that can affect the money supply of the United States. For instance, the Board can buy or sell United States Government securities, thus increasing or decreasing the amount of money in circulation. Other open-market interventions of the Federal Reserve Banks include the purchase and sale of investments such as bankers' acceptances and bills of exchange.

The Federal Reserve Board can also influence the volume of activity on the Stock Exchanges by setting margin requirements for the purchase of securities. In other words, the Federal Reserve Board can set the percentage of the market price of securities that a buyer must pay when buying stocks or bonds with a loan. Margin requirements thus limit the amount of credit that purchasers of securities may be given to finance their investment activity. By raising or lowering margin requirements, the Federal Reserve Board may limit or expand the volume of stock purchases.

Comprehension Check

A. State whether each of the following sentences is true or false based on the reading passage.

1. There are twelve Federal Reserve Banks in the United States.
2. The Board of Governors of each Federal Reserve Bank sets its own policies.
3. The actions of the Federal Reserve System affect the amount of money in circulation in the United States.
4. Federal Reserve Banks are not empowered to buy and sell investments.
5. Margin requirements set by the Federal Reserve Board limit the amount of credit available to purchasers of stocks and bonds.

B. Answer the following questions orally.

1. How many Federal Reserve Banks are there in the United States?
2. Who sets the policies of these banks?
3. How do Federal Reserve Banks extend credit to member banks?
4. How does the Board of Governors influence the money supply of the United States?
5. What can the Board of Governors do with United States Government securities?
6. What can Federal Reserve Banks buy and sell?
7. How does the Federal Reserve Board influence the volume of activity on the Stock Exchange?
8. What do margin requirements limit?
9. What are reserve requirements?
10. Which institution performs the functions of the United States Federal Reserve System in your country?

C. Composition. Write a paragraph comparing and contrasting the Federal Reserve System of the United States with the Central Bank or equivalent institution that performs this role in your own country.

Building Your Vocabulary

A. Matching. Find the words in the right-hand column that are closest in meaning to the words in the left-hand column.

1. uniform
2. market price
3. stock
4. for public sale
5. authorize
6. investment
7. mandatory
8. amount of buying and selling
9. set
10. certificate of debt

a. required
b. establish
c. bond
d. current price
e. unchanging
f. volume of activity
g. a share of corporate capital
h. open-market
i. property bought for profit
j. empower

B. **Rewriting sentences.** Rewrite each of the following sentences replacing the underlined word or words with the correct form of one of the new words of this lesson.

Model: The Board of Governors sets the <u>obligatory</u> cash ratio of holdings to liabilities.
→ The Board of Governors sets the mandatory cash ratio of holdings to liabilities.

1. Policies of the twelve Federal Reserve Banks are <u>the same everywhere</u>.
2. A group of administrators <u>fixes</u> the policies.
3. He has many <u>properties bought for profit</u>.
4. The amount of money in circulation varies with the buying and selling of <u>stocks and bonds</u>.
5. There has been a great <u>amount of buying and selling</u> on the stock exchange.

PRESENTATION

Indirect objects as subjects of passive sentences

        subject   **i.o.**
The company gave the investors information.

subject
The investors were given information by the company.

        subject   **i.o.**
The teller showed me the forms.

subject
I was shown the forms by the teller.

        subject   **i.o.**
The bank will send us a monthly statement.

subject
We will be sent a monthly statement by the bank.

Structure Practice

A. Restate each of the following sentences as a passive using the underlined indirect object as the subject.

  Model: The credit department lent Mr. Edwards $5,000.
    → Mr. Edwards was lent $5,000 by the credit department.
  1. The bank sent me information about the new interest rates.
  2. Ms. Scott will tell the board about her holdings.
  3. The bank is offering bankers' acceptances to the public.
  4. They told us there are twelve Federal Reserve Districts.
  5. The board gave the investors the data about their stocks and bonds.

B. Use each string of elements to write a passive sentence as in the model. Use the past tense.

  Model: Ms. Ferguson/give/loan/the bank
    → Ms. Ferguson was given a loan by the bank.
  1. I/show/the Stock Exchange/other investors
  2. Lisa Marlowe/offer/the necessary capital/her father
  3. The administrators/tell/market price
  4. The director/pay/the board
  5. They/inform/the bonds were sold

C. Answer the following questions using a passive voice with the indirect object of the question becoming the subject of the answer. Follow the model.

  Model: "Did the bank lend you the money?"
    "Yes, I was lent the money by the bank."
  1. Did the Federal Reserve Board sell investments to the public?
  2. Did Mr. Miller teach the students about the Federal Reserve System?
  3. Did the credit department give you the loan?
  4. Did the Board of Governors tell her about the securities?
  5. Did the company pay the directors a good salary?

Building Sentences

A. Unscramble the groups of elements to form complete sentences. Follow the model.

  Model: was lent money/Henry Henderson/by his parents
    → Henry Henderson was lent money by his parents.
  1. the data/by the administrators/we were given
  2. by the stockholders/I was offered/more securities
  3. the purchase price/by the board/they'll be told
  4. Mr. and Mrs. Rogers/by the head of the company/are sent/the stock certificates
  5. the Stock Exchange/you/by the director/will be shown

B. Select elements from columns **A, B, C** and **D** to form passive sentences with original indirect objects as subjects. Use any tense you have studied.

Model: A   B   C   D
          you   will be offered   a contract   by the company

A	B	C	D
I	sell	money	board of directors
Jane	show	the market price	the administrators
you	offer	stock certificates	the bank
Mr. Ferguson	lend	capital	Ms. Edwards
we	give	a loan	the credit department
the public	tell	the Stock Exchange	the company
the investors	send	a contract	the Federal Reserve Bank

C. Complete each of the following sentences by selecting the correct word for the blank space.

1. Policies are _____ by the board.
   a. conducted   b. set
2. It is _____ that the bank follow the policy.
   a. mandatory   b. uniform
3. Mr. Carter was _____ to sell government securities.
   a. empowered   b. performed
4. We don't want any _____ in our affairs.
   a. circulation   b. intervention
5. These operations are similar to other operations that were _____ in Latin America.
   a. limited   b. carried out

BANKING CONVERSATIONS

A. You are a member of the Board of Governors of the United States Federal Reserve System. You are asked to give a lecture about the system. Explain the following terms to the people who are listening to your lecture.
1. bill of exchange
2. open-market operations
3. reserve requirements

B. You work on the Stock Exchange in New York City. You are asked to explain certain terms to a group of prospective investors.
1. volume of activity
2. stock
3. margin requirements

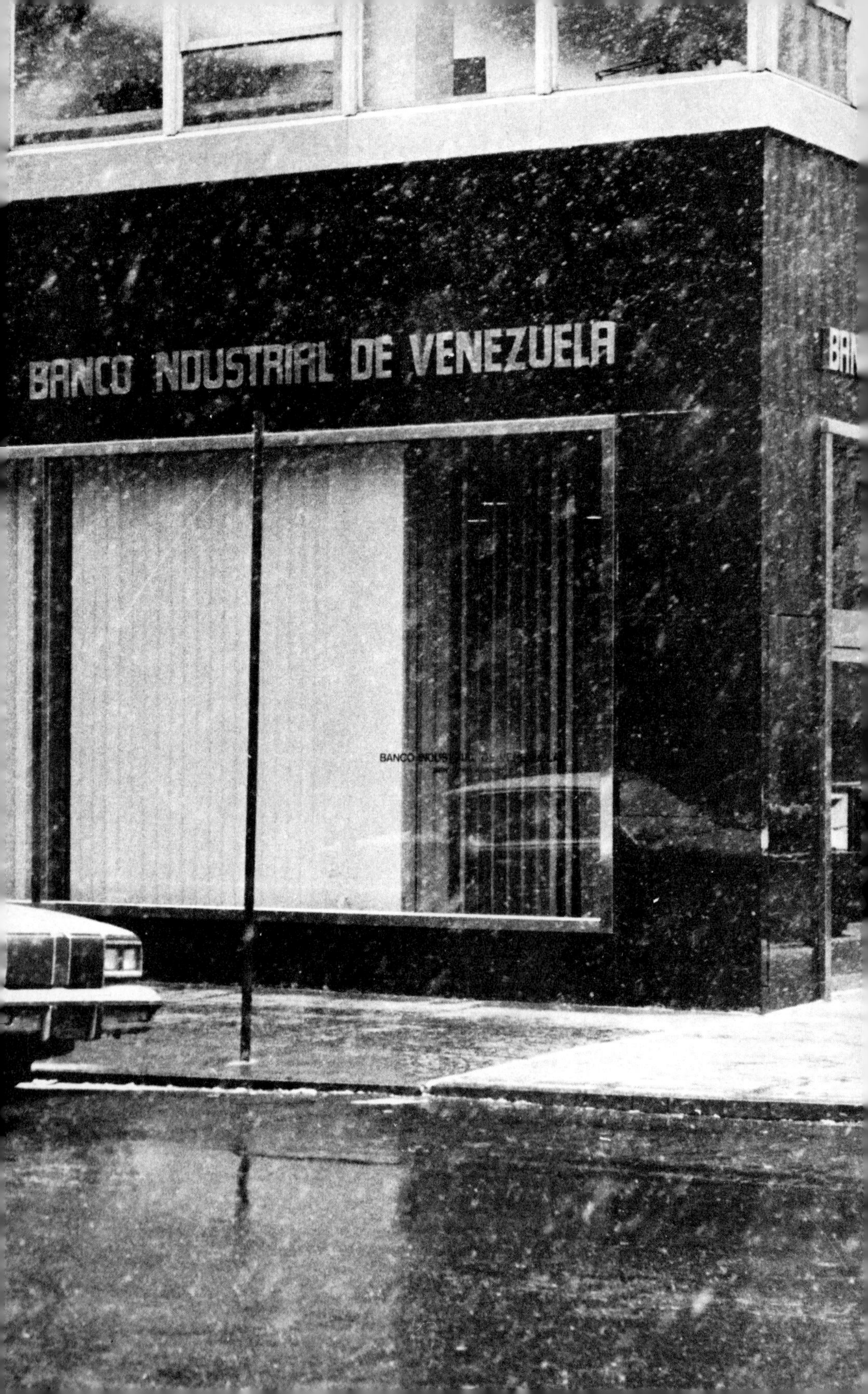
BANCO INDUSTRIAL DE VENEZUELA

LESSON 9

INTERNATIONAL BANKING FACILITIES

VOCABULARY

offshore—away from the shore; (here) across the ocean
onshore—on land; (here) in the United States
   shore—land at the edge of a river, lake or ocean
international banking facilities—branches of banks that handle international investment
Euromarket—European investment markets
ceiling—(here) upper or top limit
insurance premium—money paid for an insurance policy
competitive—(here) able to offer goods and services at current prices
access—freedom to use
sovereign risk—government action that affects banks
exchange—trading in foreign currencies
exchange controls—limits on the trading of currencies and gold
regulations—rules, orders, directions
factor—an element or circumstance
advantage—benefit, opportunity, superiority; a factor that makes one thing better than another
remove—take away, eliminate
basis point—0.1% (one-tenth of one percent)
Eurodollars—U.S. dollars held by individual people or institutions outside the United States
to pass on—to transfer, give, share

Expansion

corporate—of corporations
to invest—to place money with the hope of making a profit
investment—the money that is placed or invested; also, the property that is bought with the money
investor—the person who invests money
   Much U.S. corporate cash is at present invested in Europe.

overseas—across the ocean
subsidiary—a company controlled by another company through stock ownership
Some large corporations have many overseas subsidiaries.
exchange rate—the amount of one currency that can be bought by a unit (mark, pound, franc, dollar, yen) of another currency
policy—a) a written insurance document
b) plan, a group of decisions about how to act in certain situations
abroad—in a foreign country
Sometimes exchange rates are more favorable abroad than at home.

Vocabulary Practice

Select the answer that correctly completes each sentence.

1. Investors sometimes have problems because of government _____.
   a. access   b. regulations   c. branches
2. Many United States corporations have _____ in other countries.
   a. subsidiaries   b. basis points   c. ceilings
3. United States banks have tried to be _____ with overseas banks.
   a. offshore   b. competitive   c. corporate
4. The New York banks plan to _____ savings in costs to their clients.
   a. advantage   b. remove   c. pass on
5. Mr. Castro will have to pay a high _____ for his insurance policy.
   a. exchange rate   b. sovereign risk   c. premium

INTERNATIONAL BANKING FACILITIES
FOR NEW YORK

Note: The information in the following passage is taken from an article appearing in *Business Week*, June 29, 1981, p. 100.

As much as $250 billion in offshore funds—most of it corporate cash of United States companies—may soon move onshore as a result of the Federal Reserve Board's decision to permit banks to open international banking facilities (IBFs) in the United States after the third of December. These IBFs will be located in New York, the financial center of the United States.

These new international banking facilities will be allowed to conduct business in the $700 billion Euromarkets, but will be free of United States reserve requirements, ceilings on interest rates, and insurance premiums. Until now, in order to do business without such costs and to be competitive with foreign banks, United States banks had to set up branches abroad. Access to the IBFs will be limited to foreign clients and overseas subsidiaries of United States corporations. The establishment of the IBFs in New York should please many corporations. Many United States firms have not been happy about the idea of investing their money in places such as the Bahamas, Bahrain, or Singapore. Some corporations consider that even London is too far away for them. They feel it will be easier to work within New York.

Corporation officials also feel that sovereign risk is less in the United States than elsewhere. When investing in other countries, they worry about political problems, the danger of war, and the possibility of new taxes or exchange controls or other regulations that could make it difficult for an investor to have free access to his cash.

Time differences will also make banking and investing in New York more attractive, especially to those corporations that do a lot of business in Canada and Latin America. The six-hour time difference between London banks and New York is often very inconvenient to these corporate investors.

Another factor that will play an important role is price. Some bankers believe that the New York banks may be able to offer an advantage. If the new regulations remove reserve requirements, insurance premiums, and local taxes, then the IBFs may be able to pay 25 basis points less than the three-month Eurodollar rate for the funds that they borrow. They could pass on part of that saving to their corporate clients, who might save 5 to 10 basis points on a loan. Since the investment world is so competitive, the savings offered by the international banking facilities of New York may well attract billions of dollars from Europe to the United States.

Comprehension Check

A. State whether each sentence is true or false based on the reading.

1. The Federal Reserve Board is affecting the flow of overseas funds to the United States.
2. The international banking facilities will be set up outside of the United States.
3. The IBFs will have the problem of United States reserve requirements.
4. Many United States corporations have been afraid they would not have free access to their capital invested overseas.
5. Corporations that deal a lot with Canada and Latin America will appreciate having the IBFs in New York.
6. The IBFs will transact business in the European investment markets.
7. If the IBFs save on local taxes and insurance premiums, they could share part of that saving with their corporate clients.
8. Corporate clients could save 25 basis points on a transaction.
9. Directors of many large United States corporations believe that sovereign risk is greater in foreign countries than in the United States.
10. It is expected that about $700 billion in offshore funds may come into the United States after December 3.

B. Answer the following questions orally.

1. What advantage will the establishment of the IBFs in the United States have?
2. Why has it been difficult for U.S. banks to compete with foreign banks up until now?
3. Why have many United States corporations not been enthusiastic about investing abroad?
4. Why is New York City a good place to locate the IBFs?
5. What is the great price advantage that New York banks may be able to offer?

C. **Composition.** Write a paragraph describing how the IBFs will make United States banks more competitive with overseas banks in the Euromarkets.

Building Your Vocabulary

A. **Matching.** Find the words in the right-hand column that are closest in meaning to the words in the left-hand column.

1. branch
2. highest point
3. insurance papers
4. rules
5. 0.1%
6. currency prices
7. permission to use
8. U.S. currency in Europe

a. policy
b. basis point
c. subsidiary
d. exchange rates
e. Eurodollars
f. access
g. ceiling
h. regulations

B. **Rewriting sentences.** Rewrite each of the following sentences replacing the underlined word or words with the correct form of one of the new words of this lesson.

Model: The banks hope to attract more <u>overseas</u> funds.
→ The banks hope to attract more offshore funds.

1. New regulations will set up <u>branches of banks that handle international investments.</u>
2. There are many <u>elements</u> that make it difficult to conduct business abroad.
3. One of the new bank rules will <u>eliminate</u> reserve requirements.
4. Millions of <u>U.S. dollars</u> are held by large French corporations.
5. The <u>upper limits</u> on interest rates will be coming down.

PRESENTATION

I. Future tense

I	(I'll)	
You	(You'll)	
He	(He'll)	
She	will* (She'll)	invest in that corporation.
We	(We'll)	
They	(They'll)	

Will* I / you / he / she / we / they have access to the cash?
No, won't. (will not)

*In British English, *shall* replaces *will* in the first person singular and plural: *I shall go, we shall go.* In American English, *shall* is used in question form with *I* and *we* (shall I, shall we) to ask for instructions (Shall I fill out the form in pen or pencil?).

International Banking 85

II. *be + going to* + simple verb

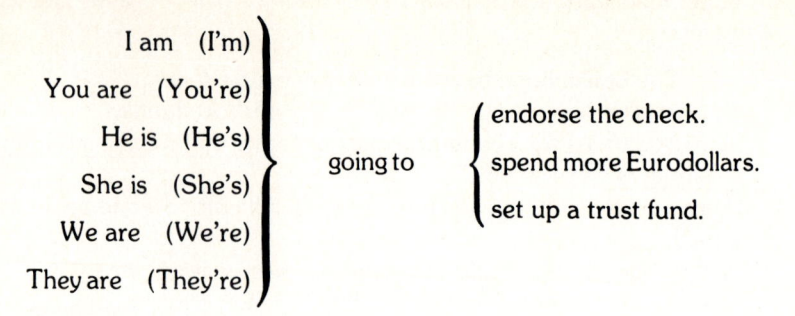

I am (I'm)		endorse the check.
You are (You're)		
He is (He's)	going to	spend more Eurodollars.
She is (She's)		
We are (We're)		set up a trust fund.
They are (They're)		

Structure Practice

A. Restate each of the following sentences, changing the verb from present to future.

   Model: He changes the regulations.
   → He will (He'll) change the regulations.
   1. You have an advantage over them.
   2. Our prices are competitive with theirs.
   3. They set up a subsidiary corporation.
   4. She looks for more investors.
   5. I consider all the factors.

B. Restate each of the following sentences in the negative.

   Model: I will work in New York.
   → I won't (I will not) work in New York.
   1. He will pass on the savings.
   2. We will pay the insurance premium.
   3. Reserve requirements will be removed.
   4. I will visit all the overseas branches.
   5. You will escape local taxes.

C. Answer each of the following questions negatively, as in the model.

   Model: Did you close your account yesterday?
   → No, I'll close it tomorrow.
   1. Did Ms. Eliot co-sign the loan yesterday?
   2. Did they go to the Stock Exchange yesterday?
   3. Did you (*pl.*) prepare the budget yesterday?
   4. Did I get the call from London yesterday?
   5. Did we receive the rules yesterday?

D. Restate each of the following sentences using the *be + going to +* simple verb construction.

    Model: We'll remove reserve requirements.
              → We're going to remove reserve requirements.
1. I'll send you the policy.
2. They'll permit banks to establish IBFs.
3. She'll do a lot of business in Canada.
4. You'll draw up a will.
5. We'll pay in monthly installments.

E. Answer each of the following questions using *shall I* or *shall we* to ask for instructions, as in the model.

    Model: "You have to go to the bank, don't you?"
              "Yes, shall I go now?"
1. You have to make an overseas call, don't you?
2. We have to cash a check, don't we?
3. You have to open a charge account, don't you?
4. We have to compute the interest, don't we?
5. You have to speak with the manager, don't you?

Building Sentences

A. **Noun compounds**. Restate each sentence by changing the underlined words to a noun compound, as in the model.

    Model: There are many facilities for banking.
              → There are many banking facilities.
1. There's a six-hour difference in time.
2. We'll pay the premiums on the insurance.
3. The officials of the corporation established the policy.
4. What is the current rate for the Eurodollar?
5. The board will remove the ceilings on interest rates.
6. The world of investment is very competitive.

B. Select elements from columns **A**, **B** and **C** to form at least eight sentences in the future. Make both affirmative and negative sentences.

A	B	C
You	invest (in)	savings
The corporation official	consider	overseas subsidiaries
We	offer	Eurodollars
I	establish	insurance premiums
Mr. and Mrs. Lee	pass on	the new regulations
Foreign clients	attract	reserve requirements
The Federal Reserve Board	earn	exchange controls
	remove	some advantages
	explain	other factors

International Banking

C. Form complete sentences referring to the future by filling in the correct forms of *be* and adding another appropriate *verb*.

Model: She (be) going to (   ) a loan.
→ She's going to apply for a loan.

1. I (   ) going to (   ) very competitive.
2. They (   ) going to (   ) an advantage.
3. The administrator (   ) going to (   ) new rules.
4. We (   ) going to (   ) offshore funds.
5. You (   ) going to (   ) business in New York.
6. Prices (   ) going to (   ) an important role.
7. It (   ) going to (   ) inconvenient for us.

READING PLUS

Now that you have completed the lesson on international banking facilities you can examine a table that shows exchange rates of some important world currencies. The figures in the table are from June 16, 1981. Before examining the table, study the following words and phrases.

spot—immediately effective; for immediate delivery
table—chart or list of details or information
format—arrangement
version—form, format, variation
bank prime—rate of interest that U.S. commercial banks charge their best corporate customers
currency—banknotes (paper money) and coin that are official in a country

After you know the meaning of each of the above items, examine the table of exchange rates and answer the questions that follow it.

Foreign exchange trader

PERCENT

	U.S. TREASURY BILLS	CERTIFICATES OF DEPOSIT U.S.	EUROMARKET	SINGAPORE	EUROMARKET TIME DEPOSITS*
SPOT	X	X	X	X	X
THREE-MONTH	13.75	16.30	16.80	17.00	17.19
SIX-MONTH	13.50	15.55	16.10	16.30	16.56
ONE-YEAR	12.80	15.25	15.60	15.90	15.13
BANK PRIME	20.00%	X	X	X	X

Data: First Boston Corp., Irving Trust Co.   As of June 16, 1981

BANKING CONVERSATIONS

A. You are the head of a United States bank. You have just heard about the Federal Reserve Board's decision to permit banks to set up IBFs in New York. Explain why you are very pleased with this ruling.

B. You are a corporation official whose company has investments in many parts of the world. You and the other corporation officials have not liked the idea of investing overseas because you feel sovereign risk is too great. Explain what is meant by sovereign risk and how it can affect your corporation.

Questions

1. How many French francs will one U.S. dollar buy?
2. How much is one British pound worth in U.S. dollars?
3. Is the precentage higher on Euromarket certificates of deposit over three months or over six months?
4. Where is the percentage on certificates of deposit the highest?
5. For what period of time is the percentage on Euromarket time deposits the lowest? What is the percentage?
6. How many Italian lira will one U.S. dollar buy?
7. How much is one Japanese yen worth in U.S. currency?

Reprinted from the June 29, 1981 issue of *Business Week* by special permission, © 1981 by McGraw-Hill, Inc., New York, NY 10020. All rights reserved.

This table has been expanded to show exchange rates in the format used by professional traders (for example, one dollar will buy 2.35 West German marks) as the version preferred by travelers (one mark is worth about 43¢).

FOREIGN UNITS PER U.S. DOLLAR (top)/U.S. DOLLARS (bottom)

GERMAN MARK	SWISS FRANC	JAPANESE YEN	CANADIAN DOLLAR	FRENCH FRANC	BRITISH POUND	ITALIAN LIRA
2.35	2.04	220	1.20	5.59	.5013	1171
.4264	.4890	.004545	.8308	.1788	1.9950	.000854
2.32	2.01	215	1.21	5.63	.4948	1190
.4315	.4980	.004661	.8274	.1776	2.0210	.000840
2.30	1.98	211	1.21	5.67	.4925	1211
.4353	.5054	.004746	.8250	.1765	2.0305	.000826
2.27	1.91	204	1.22	5.70	.4895	1252
.4403	.5222	.004891	.8230	.1754	2.0430	.000799
13.75%	6.50%	6.50%	20.00%	17.00%	13.00%	22.50%

*At London interbank offered rates

International Banking

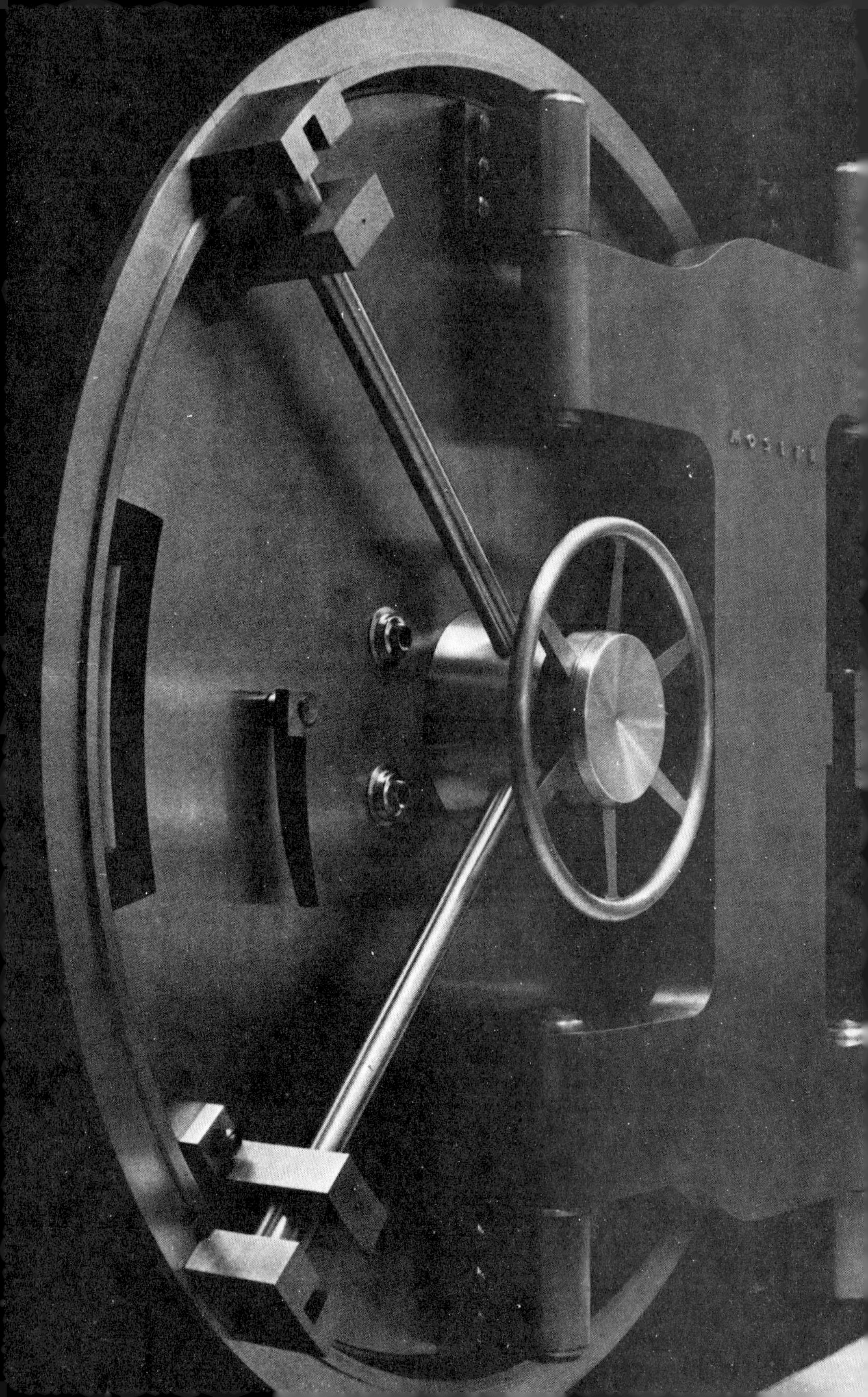

LESSON 10

THE INTERNATIONAL MONETARY FUND

VOCABULARY

International Monetary Fund (IMF)—an international fund (founded at Bretton Woods, New Hampshire, U.S.A. in 1944). The purpose of the IMF is to encourage international cooperation on money and to make payments easier between member nations.
economy—system of producing and distributing wealth
Third World—developing nations
oil—petroleum
funds—money
additional—more, increased, added
successful—that works or functions; that has the effect it is supposed to or expected to
corrective—that improves, makes better
suspicious—believing something is bad
to weaken—to get or become weak; make weak (weak: not strong)
to increase—to raise or rise
share—percentage, portion, part
loan commitment—a financial liability; term of the loan
oil-poor—that doesn't have oil (said of countries or regions)
gross national product—a measure of the total of goods and services produced by the people in one country in one year
per capita (Latin phrase that means *for each head*)—per person (per: by, for each)
basic goods—essential products
currency—banknotes (paper money) and coin that are official for buying and selling in a particular country

Expansion

standard—rule, basis, or guide for making a decision
credit standard—demands made by the lender; a test for the capacity to repay a loan
You must meet the bank's credit standards if you want a loan.

91

to project—to plan, guess in advance
deficit—lack, shortage of money
  Your budget says you have $800, but your projected expenses are $900. You're going to have a $100 deficit this month.
reform—a change to make something better; a corrective change
to impose—to make or force someone to do something
  The government imposed important economic reforms on the country.
demanding—strict, severe; insisting that rules and regulations be followed exactly
terms—requirements, demands
  The terms of the contract are very demanding.
to devalue—to lower the rate at which one currency is exchanged for another
  The government of Mexico has decided to devalue the peso.

Supplementary Vocabulary

devaluation—lowering of the rate at which one currency is exchanged for another
  The country has had three devaluations this year.
strengthen—make stronger; opposite of *weaken*
oil-rich—having a lot of oil (said of countries or regions)

Vocabulary Practice

Select the answer that correctly completes each sentence.

1. Those countries need _____ financing to establish their programs of industrialization.
   a. outstanding   b. weakening   c. additional
2. The managing director _____ that the loan will be repaid in five years.
   a. projects   b. imposes   c. persuades
3. Bankers worry that the IMF is lowering its _____.
   a. standards   b. gross national product   c. basic goods
4. Several countries have had to _____ their currency recently.
   a. borrow   b. devalue   c. increase
5. Because of high payments for oil, many oil-poor nations face big _____ in their budgets.
   a. volumes   b. deficits   c. conditionality

NEW DEVELOPMENTS AT THE INTERNATIONAL MONETARY FUND

Note: The information in the following passage is taken from *Business Week*, July 27, 1981, p. 70.

The International Monetary Fund (IMF) seems to be developing two types of credit for the economies of Third World countries. Although the IMF is lending more money than ever before, bankers are worried that credit standards of the IMF will be lowered. If this happens, then it will no longer be true that a loan from the IMF guarantees a country's creditworthiness.

It is essential that the commercial banks maintain their confidence in the programs of the IMF. These commercial banks will be financing, during 1981 and 1982, most of the projected $182 billion deficit of those developing nations that do not have their own oil. The IMF expects to lend $24 billion to those countries during this two-year period. The managing director of the Fund, Jacques de Larosière, has said that the IMF can supply only a small part of the funds that are needed by the member countries. He says that for these countries to get additional financing they must have successful programs of economic reform. The directions their programs of reform take are determined in large part by conditionality. Conditionality means changes in economic policy that the IMF imposes on borrowing nations before granting them a loan. Banks are sometimes able to persuade borrowers to adopt corrective programs in order to make it more probable that a debt will be repaid, but traditionally, the IMF has been much more powerful than individual banks in this area. Bankers, however, are now suspicious that IMF conditionality is weakening. They accept the increases in the volume of lending by the IMF, but are disturbed by the less demanding terms of IMF loans and the increasing percentage of IMF funds lent to nations with little or no commercial bank credit.

There are four developments at the IMF that worry bankers the most.
1. They do not like new IMF policies that allow countries to borrow up to six times their basic shares in the fund.
2. They are not pleased that loan commitments have been extended from one year to three.
3. The share of IMF debt held by industrial countries fell from 49% to 9% while the share of outstanding loans to oil-poor developing countries has risen from 51% to 91%.
4. 53% of the Fund's outstanding loans are to nations with gross national products of less than $700 per capita.

Here are some examples of conditions imposed on recent IMF loans. Before Uganda was given a $182 million credit in June, it had to raise its gasoline prices and the prices of basic goods. The prices of basic goods had been fixed at low levels by the Ugandan government. Zaire had to devalue its currency by 40% before being granted $1 billion in the same month. And Jamaica had to make important economic changes before getting a $619 million loan in April.

However, many bankers feel that in spite of IMF conditionality, many of the loans to the poorest countries stand very little chance of being repaid. In their opinion, the IMF should not concentrate most of its funds in loans to nations that cannot meet their loan commitments. They would like to see conditionality become stricter.

Comprehension Check

A. State whether each statement is true or false based on the reading passage.

1. Bankers are worried that the International Monetary Fund's conditionality is too demanding.
2. The IMF supplies most of the funds needed by its developing member nations who are oil-poor.
3. IMF member countries get additional financing if they have successful programs of economic reform.
4. More than half of the IMF's outstanding loans are to countries with gross national products of less than $700 per person.
5. The IMF granted Zaire a $1,000,000,000 loan in June of 1981 only after it devalued its currency by 40%.

B. Combine each group of words into a sentence that expresses information contained in the reading passage. You may add whatever words are necessary to form a grammatically correct sentence.

1. essential/commercial banks/confidence/International Monetary Fund
2. share/debt/industrial countries/fell/49%/9%
3. bankers/suspicious/conditionality/weakening
4. countries/borrow/six times/basic shares/fund
5. conditionality/changes/economic policy/imposed/IMF

C. Answer each of the following questions orally.

1. What will the commercial banks be financing during 1981 and 1982?
2. How can IMF member countries get additional financing?
3. What does the IMF impose on borrowing nations before granting them a loan?
4. What are the developments at the IMF that bankers are worried about?
5. What are some of the conditions on loans to member countries that the IMF imposed during 1981?

D. **Composition**. Write a paragraph describing how the International Monetary Fund functions and what its policies are.

Building Your Vocabulary

A. Matching. Find the words in the right-hand column that match the words closest in meaning in the left-hand column.

1. increase
2. oil
3. more
4. share
5. requirements
6. without oil
7. corrective
8. deficit
9. money
10. demanding

a. shortage of money
b. portion
c. strict
d. funds
e. raise
f. that improves
g. terms
h. petroleum
i. additional
j. oil-poor

B. Rewriting sentences. Rewrite each of the following sentences replacing the underlined word or words with the correct form of one of the new words of this lesson.

1. We're trying to <u>plan</u> how much money we'll need.
2. The new <u>regulations</u> are less <u>strict</u>.
3. The government needs IMF financing for its programs of economic <u>change</u>.
4. The poorest countries can't meet their <u>financial liabilities</u>.
5. Bankers worry that IMF conditionality <u>is becoming less strong</u>.
6. They need <u>more</u> capital for economic reform.
7. Some nations have a successful <u>system for producing and distributing wealth</u>.
8. Many of the <u>essential products</u> are very expensive in poor countries.

PRESENTATION

Comparison of adjectives and adverbs

A.

adjective	comparative form	superlative form
poor	{ poorer / less poor	{ poorest / least poor
strict	{ stricter / less strict	{ strictest / least strict
busy	{ busier / less busy	{ busiest / least busy
demanding	{ more demanding / less demanding	{ most demanding / least demanding
successful	{ more successful / less successful	{ most successful / least successful

adverb	comparative form	superlative form
successfully	more/less successfully	most/least successfully
suspiciously	more/less suspiciously	most/least suspiciously

B. Irregular comparative and superlative forms

adjective/adverb	comparative form	superlative form
good/well	better	best
bad/badly	worse	worst
little*	less	least
much	more	most
many	more	most
far	farther/further	farthest/furthest

C. Sentences with comparative constructions

This country is { poorer / less poor / more important / less important } *than* that country.

This country is *as* { poor / important } *as* that country.

This bank works { better / worse / more efficiently / less efficiently } *than* that bank.

This bank works *as* { well / efficiently } *as* that bank.

---

*When *little* means *small* its forms are *little, littler, littlest*.
We have little money, but he has less money.
We have a little house, but his house is littler than ours.

Structure Practice

A. Restate each of the following sentences, changing the adjective or adverb to the comparative form as in the model.

Model: This policy is *new*. Mr. Stone is *worried*.
→ This policy is newer. → Mr. Stone is more worried.

1. Conditionality will be *strict*.
2. Credit standards are *low* now.
3. The country's corrective program was *important*.
4. They sold their basic goods *competitively*.
5. She read the will *suspiciously*.

B. There's a major economic crisis. Answer your co-worker's questions about the latest developments using a superlative, as in the model.

Model: "Were the interest rates higher in February?"
"Yes, they were the *highest* ever."

1. Were the prices on the stock market worse yesterday?
2. Were the terms of the loan more severe that year?
3. Was he more worried about the devaluation yesterday?
4. Did the administrator speak less confidently?
5. Was the gross national product lower this year?

C. Use each string of elements to write a sentence that contains a comparative form. You may choose either *more* or *less*. Add any words necessary to make your sentence grammatically correct.

Model: I/worried/co-signer
→ I am more (less) worried than the co-signer.

1. IMF/strict/rules/banks
2. oil-rich countries/developed/oil-poor nations
3. Ms. Stewart/impose/policy/successfully/Mr. Todd
4. Uganda/expensive/goods/Zaire
5. economic changes/slowly/consumer demands
6. Great Britain/industrialized/Jamaica

D. Complete each of the following sentences by filling in the correct form of the adjective or adverb.

Model: Their stocks are good, but mine are <u>better</u>.
Their stocks are good, but mine are the <u>best</u>.
Their stocks are <u>good</u>.

1. Venezuela has much petroleum, but Mexico has ____.
2. He did the job ____, but they did it the worst.
3. The director had little power, but the manager had the ____.
4. The commercial bank was ____ away, but the savings bank was further.
5. Your corporation has done the project well, but our company has done it the ____.
6. The political problems are ____, but the taxes are worse.

The IMF **97**

E. Combine each pair of sentences into one sentence expressing equality.

> Model: Germany's prices are competitive. Japan's prices are also competitive.
> → Japan's prices are as competitive as Germany's (prices).

1. These bonds are valuable. Those bonds are also valuable.
2. Ms. Martinet spoke well. Ms. LaRosa also spoke well.
3. Their currency is strong. Our currency is also strong.
4. The IMF carried out the plan successfully. The commercial banks also carried out the plan successfully.
5. The investors are disturbed. The corporate officials are also disturbed.
6. These African nations are oil-poor. Those Asian nations are also oil-poor.
7. The place for the meeting is inconvenient. The time of the meeting is also inconvenient.

Building Sentences

A. Select elements from columns **A**, **B** and **C** to form at least ten sentences that contain either comparatives or superlatives. Add *more, less* and *than*, as needed.

A	B	C
funds	low	this year
currency	demanding	ever
conditionality	successful	in December
interest rates	good	now
credit standards	strong	last month
bankers	strict	next quarter
terms	bad	in a few weeks
the economy	worried	last year
the managing director	suspicious	two years ago
the board of governors	weak	

B. Combine each of the following two sentences into one that expresses a comparison.

> Model: Mr. Constantine has capital. Mr. Chen has more capital.
> → Mr. Chen has more capital than Mr. Constantine.
> or
> → Mr. Constantine has less capital than Mr. Chen.

1. I have $200,000 Eurodollars. You have $100,000 Eurodollars.
2. They have a deficit of $500. We have a deficit of $700.
3. Ecuador has oil. Saudi Arabia has more oil.
4. This bank has 15 branches. That bank has 20 branches.
5. The IMF is developing 14 new projects. The commercial banks are developing 12 new projects.

C. Rearrange the elements of each group to form a sentence. You may add words if necessary.
   1. adopt/programs/borrowers/corrective/sometimes
   2. outstanding/countries/loans/industrial/have/fewer
   3. need/oil-poor/financing/nations/more/developing
   4. low/prices/fixed/basic/levels/goods
   5. currency/countries/forced/many/devalue/their
   6. contract/strict/very/terms
   7. impose/policy/IMF/changes/economic
   8. banks/powerful/IMF/more/individual

D. Complete each of the following sentences by selecting either *a* or *b*.
   1. Those African nations have _____ commercial bank credit.
      a. little   b. best
   2. My terms are _____ severe than his terms.
      a. most   b. more
   3. The government will find a way to get _____ financing.
      a. farthest   b. additional
   4. We don't approve of these _____ in the volume of lending.
      a. increases   b. rise
   5. She's worried that the terms of the contract are too _____.
      a. weakening   b. demanding
   6. Although this country is _____, it has several loan commitments.
      a. oil rich   b. oil-poor

BANKING CONVERSATIONS

A. You are the managing director of the International Monetary Fund. Explain the purpose of the Fund and describe some of its most important policies with regard to loan commitments to member countries.

B. You are the head of a large commercial bank that offers financing to oil-poor developing nations. Because the policies of the International Monetary Fund affect you greatly, you are worried about some of their new directions. Discuss the developments that worry you the most and tell how they affect your transactions.

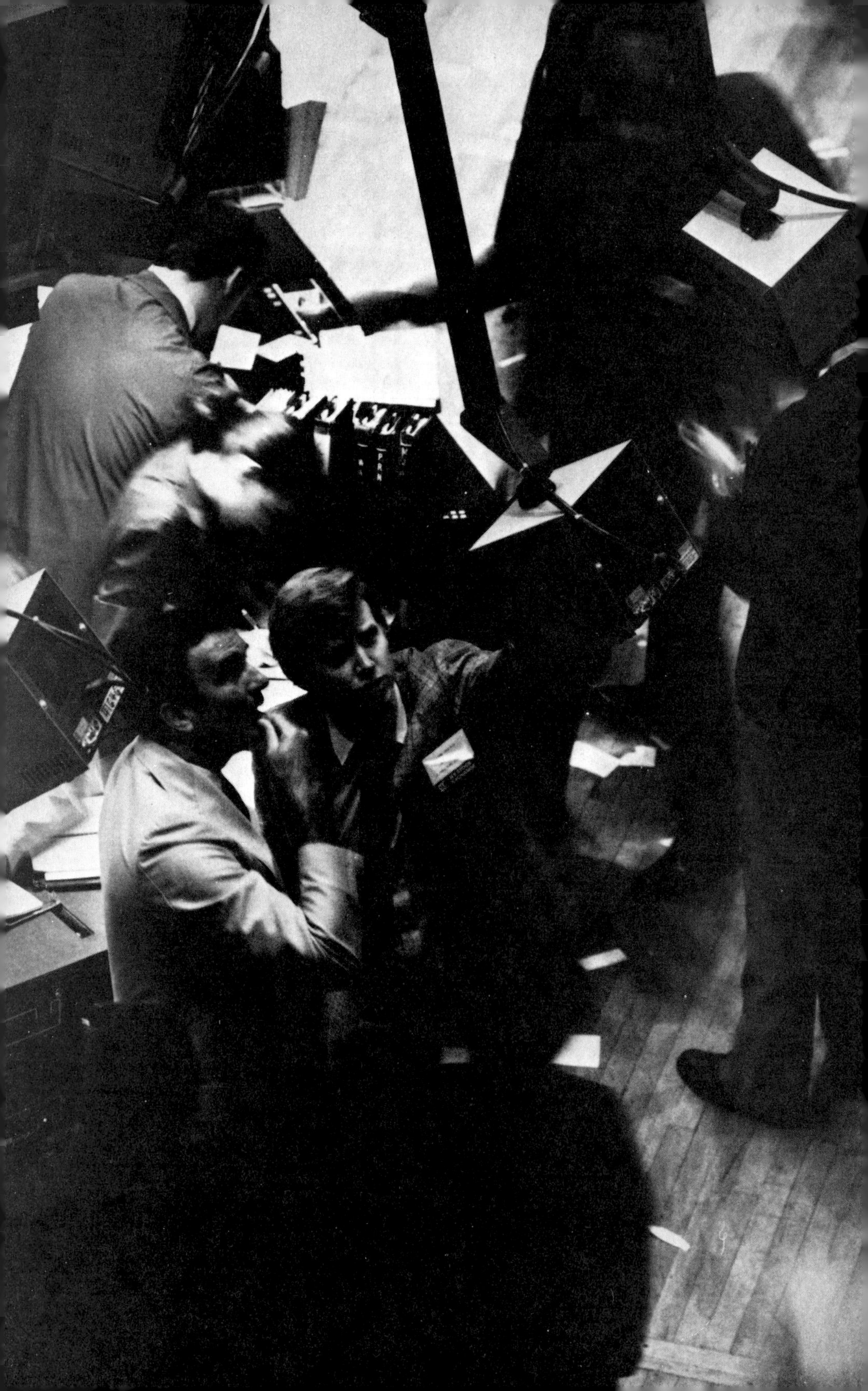

LESSON 11

INVESTMENTS (PART I)

VOCABULARY

broker (or: **stockbroker**)—an agent who buys and sells securities for other people
brokerage firm—a company of brokers
portfolio—the collection of securities owned by an investor
utilities—shares of stock in companies supplying electricity, gas, water, etc. (Note: these companies are often private, not public, in the United States.)
tax shelter—an investment made with the aim of reducing one's income tax
issue—the selling of shares by a company for the purpose of raising investment capital
speculative—taking financial risks with the hope of making large profits
price index—a number which expresses the average value of a set of related items
over-the-counter trading—buying stocks directly; that is, not on a stock exchange
merger—the uniting of two or more companies into one
dividends—the part of a company's profits paid to stockholders
active—said of stock that is bought and sold with great frequency
mutual fund—a corporation that has been formed for the purpose of investing the money of its shareholders in the securities of other companies

Expansion

common stock (in Great Britain: **ordinary shares**)—a share of stock entitling the owner to a percentage of the residual profits (not a fixed percentage, however), that is, of profits after bond holders and preferred stock holders are paid
preferred stock (in Great Britain: **preference shares**)—a share of stock that gives the owner a fixed rate of dividend
   Preferred stock holders are paid before common stock holders, but after bond holders.
taxable—that can be taxed
   Property owned by churches and schools is not taxable.

Dow Jones Industrial Average—average price of a selected group of industrial stocks on the Wall Street Stock Exchange (New York City)
point—a standard unit of value (e.g. $1.00) used to state current prices
The Dow Jones Industrial Average dropped 12 points today.
split—the division of a share of stock into two shares
Companies split stock in order to reduce the value of each share and thus make their stock more attractive to investors.
municipal bonds—issue of bonds by the government of a city
tax-exempt—not taxable
Interest payments to municipal bondholders are tax-exempt.
commodities—raw materials such as rubber or agricultural products such as coffee, wheat or livestock (animals)
futures—the purchase or sale of commodities on a specified future date
Commodities and foreign currency are popular types of futures investments.

Supplementary Vocabulary

speculate—to take financial risks with the hope of making large profits
speculation—the taking of financial risks with the hope of making large profits

Vocabulary Practice

Select the answer that correctly completes each sentence.

1. The two largest utility companies just entered into a _____.
   a. commodity   b. merger   c. tax shelter
2. My _____ will advise me about selling some of my stocks.
   a. legatee   b. credit manager   c. broker
3. Many people buy municipal bonds because they are _____.
   a. active   b. tax-exempt   c. taxable
4. Since the stock _____, I earn greater _____.
   a. split/dividends   b. trade/mutual funds
   c. future/industrial averages
5. Carol wants our brokerage firm to help her with her _____.
   a. index   b. portfolio   c. profile
6. Mr. Rowinsky can't afford to be a _____ investor.
   a. preferred   b. common   c. speculative
7. The city is selling _____ in order to pay off its debts.
   a. municipal bonds   b. commodities   c. mutual funds
8. Mr. and Mrs. D'Angelo bought 20 shares of _____ because they didn't want a fixed rate of dividend.
   a. securities   b. common stock   c. preferred stock

INVESTMENTS (PART ONE)

Phil O'Brien and his colleague Carol Levine are discussing how to invest money.

Carol   Phil, I just heard about your aunt Katherine's death. I am so sorry.

Phil   Thanks, Carol. We'll really miss her. She was so kind to the whole family. You know, she even left Barbara and me a large sum of money in her will.

Carol   What do you plan to do with the money? You might want to talk to Jeff Hunter, my broker, about investing some of it. As a broker, he can help you. The brokerage firm he works for is one of the best in the country.

Phil   That's a wonderful idea. I already have a small stock portfolio. Barbara and I own some common and preferred stocks in utilities and four other large companies.

Carol   I'm sure Mr. Hunter would be able to advise you about your taxable income. You know that you'll have to pay estate taxes on the inheritance. Perhaps he can suggest some tax shelters for you.

Phil   I do study all the new stock issues and I watch the Dow Jones industrial average carefully as it goes up or down a few points. However, I don't think that I have enough money to be a speculative investor, Carol.

Carol   Well, my broker can give you the latest information in all areas of the stock market, not just in investment for speculation. He knows all about price indexes, the latest over-the-counter trading figures, corporate mergers, stock splits, and so on.

Phil   I will speak with him because I'd like to increase my dividends from stocks. Maybe he'll be able to suggest some currently active stocks that I might want to invest in. Does his firm also handle municipal bonds and mutual funds?

Carol   I'm sure it does. Municipal bonds have always been popular because the money you earn on them is tax-exempt. Mr. Hunter can also advise you on buying commodities on the futures market.

Phil   I'll call Jeff Hunter this week to talk about investing. Do you have his telephone number?

Carol   Yes, here it is. It's 738-8492. I think you'll be very satisfied with his advice.

Comprehension Check

A. State whether each statement is true or false based on the information in the dialogue.

1. Phil O'Brien wants to invest the legacy his aunt left him.
2. As a broker, Carol Levine will help Phil with his investments.
3. Phil and Barbara O'Brien already have an investment portfolio.
4. Phil studies the stock market.
5. Phil feels he can now take great financial risks.
6. Jeff Hunter knows about all aspects of the stock market.

7. Phil hopes to increase his dividends from stocks.
8. The earnings on municipal bonds are taxable.
9. Carol thinks Mr. Hunter's brokerage firm handles mutual funds.
10. Jeff Hunter doesn't know about buying commodities on the futures market.

B. Answer each of the following questions orally.

1. Why do you think Phil and Barbara O'Brien may need a tax shelter?
2. What do the O'Briens have in their portfolio?
3. What does Phil watch in studying the stock market?
4. Why isn't Phil interested in speculation?
5. What are some of the things that Jeff Hunter can inform Phil about?
6. What kinds of securities does Mr. Hunter's brokerage firm handle?

C. **Composition.** Write a paragraph in which you describe different types of securities that an investor might have in his portfolio.

Building Your Vocabulary

A. **Matching**. Find the words in the right-hand column that are closest in meaning to the words in the left-hand column.

1. uniting of companies
2. brokerage firm
3. take financial risk
4. utilities
5. split
6. buying stocks directly
7. raw materials
8. investment to reduce taxes
9. portfolio
10. not taxable

a. a collection of securities
b. commodities
c. merger
d. tax shelter
e. tax-exempt
f. speculate
g. the gas and electric companies
h. over-the-counter trading
i. company of brokers
j. division of a share of stock

B. **Rewriting sentences.** Rewrite each of the following sentences replacing the underlined word or words with the correct form of one of the new words of this lesson.

1. These stocks are <u>frequently bought and sold</u>.
2. Your <u>agent</u> will be able to sell those securities.
3. Are they going to buy more shares in <u>the gas and water companies</u>?
4. When the stock <u>was divided,</u> we bought more shares in the company.
5. The stockholders received large <u>profits</u> from the corporation.
6. How many <u>units</u> did the Dow Jones industrial average fall today?
7. New York City issued <u>city government securities</u> in order to finance street repairs and subway construction.
8. Deborah Adams plans to <u>take a big financial risk</u> in the stock market this year.

PRESENTATION

Negative and indefinite words

affirmative statements & questions	negatives	questions & negatives
sometimes	never	ever
someone, somebody	no one, nobody	anyone, anybody
something	nothing	anything
some + noun	no + noun	any + noun
some	none	any
either . . . or . . .	neither . . . nor . . .	(either) . . . or . . .
also, too	neither	either

Example sentences:

Mary is <u>sometimes</u> here.
Is John <u>ever</u> here?
Is John here <u>sometimes</u>?
No, he's <u>never</u> here.   or   No, he isn't <u>ever</u> here.

Question formation and response:

He wants <u>something</u>.
Do you want <u>something</u>?
Do you want <u>anything</u>?
No, I don't want <u>anything</u>.

Linda's going. Bill's going <u>too</u>.
John isn't going. I'm not going <u>either</u>. <u>Neither</u> are you.

I know <u>someone</u> at the bank.
Do they know <u>someone</u> at the bank?
Do they know <u>anyone</u> at the bank?
No, they don't know <u>anyone</u> at the bank.

Investments (Part I)   **105**

I have some new checks.

Do you need some / any new checks?

No, I don't need any new checks.

He has some.

Do you want some? / any?

No, I don't want any.

Structure Practice

A. Answer each of the following questions with an affirmative response, then with a negative one, as in the model.

Model: "Do you need some data?"
"Yes, I need some."
"No, I don't need any."

1. Do you and your husband own some shares in mutual funds?
2. Did they buy some preferred stocks?
3. Will I find some good brokerage firms there?
4. Did Ms. Levine know about some corporate mergers?
5. Can we sell some commodities?
6. Is Barbara O'Brien investing in any utility companies?
7. Did you get some capital?
8. Will he distribute some property?
9. Were there some stock splits last month?
10. Can I give you some names of executors?

B. Rewrite each of the following sentences negatively. Use the appropriate negative word in each case.

Model: There are some brokers in the office.
→ There are no brokers in the office.
or
There aren't any brokers in the office.

1. There are some over-the-counter trading figures.
2. We sometimes visit the Stock Exchange.
3. Somebody has audited these accounts.
4. Either Mr. O'Brien or Ms. Levine will co-sign the loan.
5. I work in that brokerage firm also.
6. Anyone can be named as their agent.
7. Barbara O'Brien knows about securities too.
8. You sometimes check the Dow Jones average.
9. They'll need some tax shelters.
10. The McNeils have either stocks or bonds in their portfolio.

C. Rewrite each of the following negative sentences as in the model. Remember that both sentences, the original one and the one you write, have the same meaning.

Model: There isn't any money in the checking account.
→ There's no money in the checking account.

1. That bank doesn't extend any credit.
2. There aren't any price indexes in today's paper.
3. There aren't any fees for those services.
4. We don't receive any dividends.
5. There isn't any government intervention.
6. There isn't any time to draw up a will.
7. She doesn't have any shares in the corporation.
8. I don't know any executors.
9. Mr. Navarra doesn't have any holdings in that country.
10. The city hasn't issued any municipal bonds.

D. Answer each of the following questions as in the model.

Model: "Do you have any common stocks?"
"No, none."

1. Do you receive any dividends?
2. Did the board set some new policies?
3. Will they buy some utilities?
4. Did the teller have any customers?
5. Did that company issue any stocks this month?

Building Sentences

A. Organize the following strings of elements into sentences as in the model. Use the past tense.

Model: share/nobody/buy/any
→ Nobody bought any shares.
1. either/speculate/never/Phil
2. the merger/ever/no one/understand
3. visit/sometimes/too/the stock exchange/I
4. she/has/nor/a portfolio/neither/he
5. clients/brokers/see/some/no
6. some/there are/splits/stock
7. dividends/investors/get/no/some
8. the market/always/study/we/carefully

B. Select elements from columns **A, B, C** and **D** to make at least ten sentences. Be sure the sentences make sense. You may make the verbs of column **B** either affirmative or negative. Adjust the word order as necessary.

A	B	C	D
Someone	buy	any	municipal bonds
The brokers	own	some	securities
Mr. O'Brien	want	also	common stock
You	sell	never	futures
Carol	receive	ever	a merger
I	have	always	over-the-counter trading
The brokerage firm	need	neither/nor	the price indexes
Some shareholders	study	either/or	dividends
Nobody	prefer		shares
We	look for		investments
			stock splits

C. Complete each of the following sentences by selecting the correct word for the blank space.

1. There was _____ rise in the interest rate.
   a. no   b. none
2. He _____ drew up the will.
   a. never   b. ever
3. There isn't _____ money held in trust for them.
   a. no   b. any
4. _____ we need our broker's advice.
   a. sometimes   b. never
5. Either Jack _____ Al works in a Federal Reserve Bank.
   a. or   b. nor
6. I haven't seen _____ either.
   a. anyone   b. nobody

7. Did they _____ arrive at the meeting?
   a. never   b. ever
8. Ms. Wilson has 50 shares, but Ms. Wong has _____.
   a. none   b. some
9. We didn't have _____ time to meet the administrators.
   a. some   b. any
10. The board wanted _____ stock splits nor mergers.
    a. either   b. neither

BANKING CONVERSATIONS

A. You are a broker in a large brokerage firm. One of your clients has come to see you to discuss how he should invest his money. Tell him what types of securities are available and why you recommend certain ones over others.

B. You are an investor in the stock market. Describe the securities you have in your portfolio and explain how you decide what to buy and sell.

READING PLUS

Now that you have completed the lesson on investments in the stock market you can read the following sample of stock listings on the New York Stock Exchange (as seen in *The New York Times*, September 18, 1981). First study the following words and abbreviations.

Div—the current annual dividend per share
pf—preferred stock
Yld—yield (or the percentage return) represented by the annual dividend at the current stock price
PE—refers to the price-earnings ratio, that is, the number of times by which the company's latest 12-month earnings must be multiplied to obtain the current stock price
Sales 100's—refers to the volume of shares in consolidated trading. Thus, 150 in the sales column would mean 15,000 shares traded.
52-Week High and Low columns—the highest and the lowest price of the stock in consolidated trading during the preceding 52 weeks
High, Low and Last columns—refer to the day's trading prices
Chg—the difference (plus, minus, or no change) between the day's last reported price and the previous closing price
S—indicates a split or stock dividend of 25% or more has been paid
e—special or extra dividend declared or paid in the preceding 12 months

Now read the sample stock listing and answer the questions that follow it.

THE NEW YORK TIMES, SUNDAY, JANUARY

New York Stock Excha

CONSOLIDATED TRADING / WEEK ENDED FRIDAY, JANUARY 21,

Bonds	Cur. Yld	Sls in $1,000	High	Low	Last	Net Chg.
BenCp 13.65s87	14.4	308	95	94½	95	+ ¼
BenCp 9s05	9.0	41	100	99¾	100	- ¾
BenCp 13⅝91	13.0	8	104¼	102⅝	102⅝	- 3⅜
BenNJ 7¾84	8.0	37	97⅜	97⅜	97⅜	+ ⅜
Berky 5¾86	cv	1	72⅝	72⅝	72⅝	+ ¼
BethSt 4½90	7.9	50	58½	57¼	57¼	- ⅛
BethSt 5.4s92	9.4	15	57¼	56¼	57¼	+ 2¼
BethSt 6⅞99	12.3	74	58	56	56	+ 1
BethSt 9s00	13.0	48	69½	68¾	69	+ ⅜
ethSt 8.45s05	13.1	273	65	63¾	64¾	+ ⅞
ethSt 8⅜01	13.1	122	63⅞	63	[illegible]	
igT 8.55s01	10.3	7	83⅛	[illegible]		
igT 8½06	cv	143	88½			
kD 8.45s85	8.8	32	96½			
eing 8⅞06	cv	1941	102			
isC 9.9s86	10.2	35	98			
isC 10.45s90	11.0	270	95⅜	[illegible]		
rdn 8½04	11.3	146	75¾	75½		
rdn 9⅝09	11.4	20	82½	81¾		
rW 7⅞s91	9.8	2	80	80		
W 7½s93	10.1	1	74⅜	74⅜		
W 8⅜86	9.1	10	93	92½		
gW d6s01	11.1	60	54⅝	54		
W 5½s92	8.5	1	64⅞	64⅞		
oM 6s70f	...	10	155	155	[illegible]	
os 4½70f	...	2	170	170	170	
E 9¼07	12.6	35	73½	73½	[illegible]	
Jn 6¼92	8.8	13	70⅝	70⅝	70⅝	
Jn 9⅛95	11.1	8	81⅞	81⅞	81⅞	
Sh 9¼05	cv	112	72¼	70	[illegible]	
F 12⅞87	12.6	5	102	102	102	
E 9s99	11.3	60	79⅝	79⅝	79⅝	
E 7¾83	7.8	50	99½	99 7-16	99½	
a 6s90	cv	30	59¼	59⅛	59¼	+
nd 5s91	cv	51	75	75	75	-
o 8½96	11.0	20	78¾	77⅝	77⅝	+
o 12⅞05	13.1	41	102¾	98⅜	98⅜	-
10¾87	10.8	91	100⅞	100	100	-
11½10	12.7	10	90⅝	90⅝	90⅝	+ 1
10¼97	16.3	371	64⅛	63	63	- 1⅛
85s01	9.2	10	85⅝	85⅝	85⅝	......
¾98	15.0	7	87⅛	85¼	85¼	- 2¾
8s07	cv	134	113½	105¾	107½	......
95	11.2	17	84¾	84½	84½	- ¼
86	8.6	17	91⅛	91⅛	91⅛	- 1
s93	10.4	2	84½	84½	84½	+ 3
08	12.2	13	72	72	72	......
09	12.5	25	79	77¼	77¼	- ¼
½05	12.2	20	94½	93	94½	+ 2⅜
87	13.8	15	112⅜	112	112	......
95	11.3	5	75⅜	75⅜	75⅜	+ ⅜
7	14.5	1	103¾	103¾	103¾	+ 1¾
89	16.6	11	110	110	110	......
½90	13.3	146	93⅞	92⅝	93⅞	+ 1¾
¼97	14.3	28	80	78⅝	78⅝	- ⅜
s94	14.1	56	85⅞	84⅛	85	+ 1
½00	14.7	24	86⅛	85⅛	85⅛	- 2⅜
⅞90	10.0	5	98⅞	98⅞	98⅞	+ ⅞
rp	11.6	114	35	34⅜	34⅜	......
¾06	12.8	55	102	99¼	100	- 2
02	11.7	15	66⅜	66	66	+ 1⅛
88	cv	19	97	95	97	+ 2
00	11.8	9	78⅛	77⅝	77⅝	+ 1⅜
s03	11.6	5	70	70	70	+ 1¼
7s10	12.6	5	101	101	101	+ ½
6	10.9	4	74½	74½	74½	+ 2
8	10.6	35	73⅛	73⅛	73⅛	+ ⅛
½92	12.7	12	82⅝	82⅝	82⅝	+ ½
94	cv	45	70	69	69¼	- ¾
92	7.8	6	68⅞	68	68	+ ¼
	8.9	30	77	76¼	77	- 1
	11.3	5	77¾	77¾	77¾	+ ¾
	cv	99	96⅝	95½	96	- 2
8	13.5	29	109½	109½	109½	......
7	12.8	55	106⅝	104½	104½	......
O	14.5	72	79½	78½	79½	+ 1¼
N	14.5	104	79¾	79	79½	+ ½
	cv	5	73	73	73	+ 1
	cv	14	66	66	66	......

BOND VOLUME

(PAR VALUE)	1983	1982
Monday	$ 40,302,000	$ 21,[illegible]
Tuesday	40,574,00[illegible]	
Wednesday ..	[illegible]	
Thursday		

52-week High	Low	Stock	Div	Yld %	PE Ratio	Sales 100's	High	Low	Last	Chg.
60⅛	45	ATT	5.40	9.6	7	4250	56¾	56	56⅜	....
18⅜	12¾	ColgP	1.12	7.6	7	821	14⅞	14⅜	14¾	+¼
113¼	80¼	Digital		....	13	1450	89¾	87⅛	87⅜	−1⅝
44⅜	31	Exxon S	3.00	9.5	4	4267	32¼	31⅝	31⅝	−¼
35⅝	26⅜	Gillette	2.10	7.6	8	604	28⅛	27⅝	27⅝	−½
28⅝	23½	Goodrich pf	3.12	12.7	...	3	24⅞	24⅝	24⅝	−⅛
52¼	35	Hilton	1.60	4.3	9	1821	38⅜	37⅜	37⅜	−⅞
72¾	53⅜	IBM	3.44	6.4	9	5516	55⅛	53½	54⅛	−¾
37⅝	24	PepsiCo	1.46	4.8	9	1184	32¼	30¼	30⅜	−2
55⅝	37½	Raytheon S	1.2	3.1	11	525	39¼	38⅞	38⅞	−¼
20¾	14½	Sears	1.36	8.6	7	3432	16⅜	15⅝	15⅞	−½
26⅛	13⅞	SONY Cp	.13e	.7	13	7943	18	17⅝	17⅞	+⅜
37⅝	24⅜	Squibb	1.20	4.3	11	705	28⅜	27⅞	27⅞	−⅝
35¼	21	USSteel	2.00	7.2	3	1807	28⅞	27⅝	27⅝	−1⅛

12-month High	Low	Bonds	Cur. Yld	Sls in $1,000	High	Low	Last	Net Chg.
							[illegible]⅛	- ⅜
							88	......
				67	76¾	74	74	- 1
			13.1	37	69⅝	68¾	68¾	+ ¾
		CnPw 8⅞07	13.2	98	68¼	67	67	- ¾
	50⅛	CnPw 8⅝07	13.3	12	66	64¾	64¾	- 2½
69½	55⅛	CnPw 9s08	12.9	171	69½	68⅞	69½	+ ¾
40½	21	CtlAir 3½92	cv	78	40½	38⅝	40½	+ 1½
91	68¼	CtlGp 8½90	9.9	40	86	86	86	+ 1⅞
100⅛	97	CtlGp 11⅛89	11.2	13	100⅛	99	99	- ½
101¾	95⅝	Ct IlCp 11.80s89	11.9	34	99⅝	99½	99½	- ½
94⅜	79¾	Ct IC 8½85	9.1	10	93¼	93¼	93¼	- 1⅛
65¾	48⅛	CtlOil 4½91	6.8	33	65¾	63⅞	65¾	+ ¾
84½	62⅝	CtlOil 9⅛s99	10.9	5	83½	83½	83½	- 1
83½	58¼	CtlOil 8⅞01	11.0	5	81	81	81	- 1
100⅛	93½	CtlTl 10½83	10.5	47	100	99 13-16	100	+ 3-16
76⅜	61⅛	CtlDat 5½87	7.2	1	76⅜	76⅜	76⅜	+ 1
86	69	CoopL 10½92	12.2	15	86	86	86	......
186½	95	CoopL 12s07	cv	33	186½	175	182¾	+ 14¼
96	85⅝	CrnPd 4⅝83	4.9	1	95 9-32	95 9-32	95 9-32	- 23-32
111	106½	CornG 8¼07	7.7	85	108½	107	107	- 3
222	177½	Crane 5s93	cv	2	207¼	207¼	207¼	+ 22¼
62	50	Crane 7s93	11.5	11	62	61	61	+ ¼
60½	48	Crane 7s94	12.1	71	60½	57⅛	58	- 1
95	83¾	Crane 8s85	8.5	3	94	94	94	......
88	69½	Crane 10½94	12.1	4	87	87	87	+ ½
79	59	CrdF 8s92	10.4	64	78¾	77	77¼	- 1¾
92	68½	CrdF 8¾88	9.5	136	92	84⅜	92	+ 9½
95	72½	CrdF 10¼89	11.0	9	95	93⅛	93⅛	+ 3⅛
39⅝	27¾	CrdF zr90s	...	38	39⅝	39	39⅝	+ 1½
104	102	CrdF 13⅞92	13.3	30	104	104	104	+ 2
75	55¾	CrocN 5¾96	cv	17	72	72	72	+ 1
72⅝	54¼	CrocN 8.6s02	12.0	4	72⅛	71⅜	71⅜	- ¾
77	54⅜	CrwnZ 8⅞00	12.3	12	71⅞	71⅞	71⅞	- 1⅛
76½	57	CrwnZ 9¼05	12.7	6	73	73	73	+ 2¾
75⅜	56⅛	Crucbl 6⅞92	10.9	33	63	60	63	......
87	62⅛	Culb 11½05	13.6	33	84¼	83	84¼	+ 1¼
77	55	CumE 8⅞95	11.7	1	76⅛	76⅛	76⅛	......
98½	82	CyprM 8¾85	9.1	5	96½	96½	96½	+ ¼
67⅝	65¼	Dana 6s91	8.9	1	67⅝	67⅝	67⅝	......
64	46	Dana d5⅞06	cv	78	64	63⅜	63½	......
86	61	Dart 4¼97	cv	52	86	86	86	......
86	46¾	Datpnt 8⅞06	cv	312	69½	68½	68¾	- ¼
60	42½	Dayc 5¾94	cv	86	59⅞	58	59	+ ½
65	47	Dayc 6s94	cv	22	64½	62	62⅜	+ ⅜
83	54¾	Dayc 6¼96	cv	43	76½	75	76¼	- ½

12-month High	Low	Bonds	Cur. Yld	Sls in $1,000	High	
77⅝	52¼	FrdC 9⅜01	12.6	94	77⅝	[illegible]
91⅜	68⅛	FrdC 8⅝86	9.5	93	91⅜	[illegible]
74	49	rdC 9⅛01	12.6	59	73	[illegible]
		rdC 8.1s84	8.5	265	95⅞	[illegible]
		rdC 8¼88	10.1	328	82⅞	80
		dC 8⅜01	12.4	52	69	67
		C 7⅞89	10.1	309	80⅛	77
		C 7.85s88	9.5	65	83	82
		8⅜02	12.3	86	68½	66
		8½02	12.2	83	69⅞	69
		8⅜84	8.6	191	97⅞	97
		8½88	9.9	27	85⅞	85
		9s84	9.1	219	99⅞	98
		¾90	10.8	79	82⅞	79
		½85	9.8	469	97¾	96
		5s89	11.1	120	87	86
		1⅞83	11.8	106	100½	100
		.60s87	12.4	375	102½	100
		6s94	cv	9	137	136
		06	cv	155	108¼	105
		01	cv	18	144	140
			7.8	3	77	77
			cv	160	78⅞	77
			9.2	19	87	86
			8.5	120	83	82
			13.4	206	71½	69
			13.3	72	74⅛	72
			14.6	6	112	112
			14.1	7	85	83
			15.0	10	98⅛	98
		GTE 10½07	cv	239	108	106
85	64½	GTE 10s2000	12.3	10	81	81
101½	77	Gelco 14⅝99	14.6	251	101½	99
105	81½	Gelco 14s01	cv	152	101¼	100
63½	50¼	GnATr 5¾99	cv	184	63½	61
74½	53½	GnEl 5.3s92	7.5	120	73⅛	70
82	57½	GnEl 7½96	9.4	80	81½	79
84	59¼	GnEl 8½04	10.2	236	83¾	82
100	88¼	GEIC 8.65s84	8.8	25	99⅛	98 25-32
95½	77⅜	GEICr 8¼86	8.7	23	95½	94
92	68¾	GEICr 7⅝88	8.3	60	92	89
80	56	GEICr 8¼97	10.4	26	79	79
99¾	88½	GEICr 9⅛84	9.2	125	99¼	99
99⅛	79¼	GEICr 9¾87	9.9	550	99⅛	98
104⅝	85½	GEICr 11⅜88	11.4	10	103½	103
104	81⅞	GEICr 11½90	11.2	12	104	103
102⅞	72	GEICr 11¾05	11.6	36	101	99
109	90	GEICr 13⅝91	12.7	15	107⅝	107
97	75½	GFood 8⅞90	9.1	68	97	95
97⅜	86⅛	GFood 7½84	7.7	5	97⅜	97
112	96	GFood 14⅝89	13.0	3	111	111
66½	48⅛	GHost 6s90f	9.0	5	66½	65
66½	48⅛	GHost 7s94	10.5	92	66½	65
84¼	62½	GMills 8⅞95	10.6	9	84	84
77	53½	GMills 8s99	10.6	31	75½	74
60	51	GMills zr88s	...	220	60	58
99 7-32	90¼	GMA 4⅝83	4.7	5	99 7-32	99 7-32
88	70½	GMA 4½85	5.1	71	88	86
		GMA 4½85r	5.2	10	87	87
85⅜	68⅛	GMA 4⅝86	5.4	182	85⅜	83
81	61	GMA 4⅞87	6.1	39	81	79
82¾	61	GMA 6¼88	7.6	174	82⅜	81
80⅞	57⅛	GMA 7⅛90	8.9	133	80⅞	79
81⅜	58	GMA 8s93	9.9	188	81⅜	78
77⅞	54¼	GMA 7¾94	10.1	9	77⅞	76
75⅛	52	GMA 7¼95	9.9	95	74⅝	73
78⅞	55⅜	GMA 7⅛92	9.5	101	78⅜	75
75	51⅛	GMA 7.85s98	10.7	54	74⅜	73
81	56¾	GMA 8⅞99	11.5	30	79½	77
95⅞	77⅞	GMA 8⅝s85	9.0	105	95¾	94
99⅝	85⅝	GMA 8⅛s84	8.2	124	99	97
79⅝	55⅞	GMA 8¾s00	11.3	29	79⅝	77
94⅝	74¼	GMA 8⅛86A	8.6	85	94⅛	93
94⅜	76	GMA 8⅛86J	8.6	53	94⅜	92
79⅞	55	GMA 8¾s01	11.6	50	79	75
96¾	73⅜	GMA 8.15s86	8.7	60	93⅞	93
78½	55¼	GMA 8⅛96	10.5	25	77½	76
91	70¾	GMA 7.35s87	8.1	117	91	90
73¾	51	GMA 8s02	11.1	4	72	72

Questions

1. Which company shows the highest price of stock during the preceding year? And the lowest price?
2. Which company pays the highest current annual dividend per share? And the lowest?
3. Which company gives the highest yield (percentage return)?
4. Which company has the lowest price-earnings ratio?
5. Which company shows the largest volume of shares traded (Sales 100's)? And the lowest?
6. Which companies show a rise in the day's last reported trading prices as compared to the previous closing prices? How many points did they rise?
7. Which companies show the greatest change downward between the day's last reported prices and the previous closing prices? How many points did they fall?
8. Did any stocks neither rise nor fall? Which ones?
9. Do any companies show a split or stock dividend of 25% or more? Which ones?
10. Which company shows figures for preferred stock only? What is the difference between the day's last reported price and the previous closing price for that stock?
11. Which company declared or paid a special or extra dividend in the preceding 12 months?
12. If you had to purchase shares in five of the companies listed, which ones would you select? Why would you choose them?

Investments (Part I) **111**

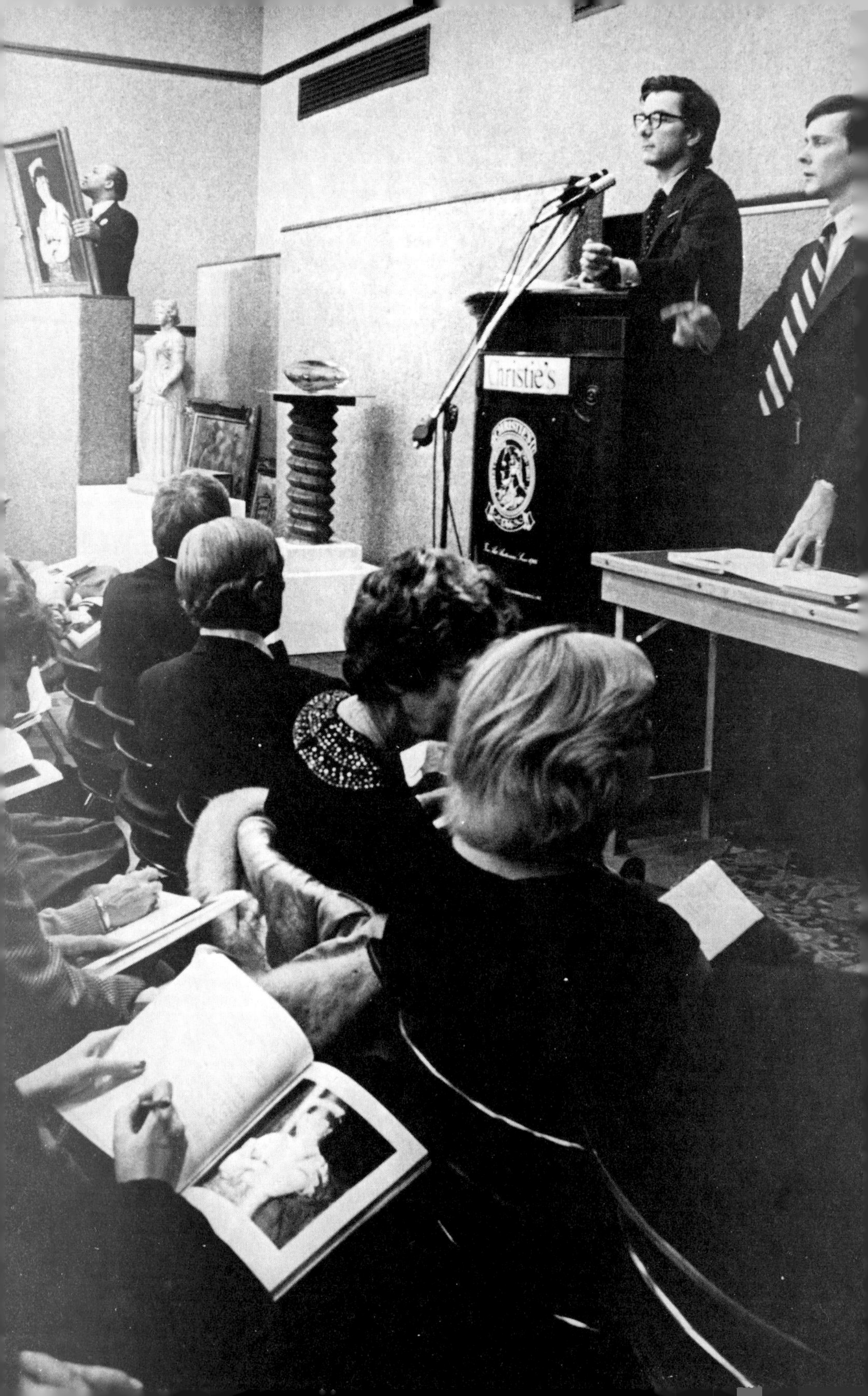
Christie's

LESSON 12

INVESTMENTS (PART II)

VOCABULARY

yield—rate of return on an investment
growth rate—percentage at which property increases in value
option—choice, alternative
bullish—said of the stock market when prices are rising
bearish—said of the stock market when prices are falling
slowdown—a decrease in industrial production and in other economic activity
inflation—a process of rising prices
double-digit (**digit** = number)—an amount having two digits, such as *17*
data processing—machines that handle information
high technology—scientific advances applied to new devices, such as computers, calculators, etc.
earnings—yield; income (money earned) on an investment or in a business
bargain—an item bought at a price that the buyer considers low
bargain-hunters—said of investors who buy stocks when prices are low
  (**to hunt**—to chase animals for food; [here] to search for eagerly)
collectibles—items such as works of art, stamps, or coins (see below) that can be collected, especially for investment purposes
works of art—paintings or sculpture (statues)
dealer—person conducting business transactions; for example, a trader, a storekeeper, a broker
bid—offer of money by a buyer for the purchase of something
auction—sale of property to the person whose bid is the highest
commission—payment for the services of an agent or broker, usually a percentage of the value of the transaction

Expansion

strategy—plan of action
recession—period of temporary economic decline and unemployment (joblessness)
  The government will reveal new strategies designed to avoid a recession.
to appreciate—to increase in value
  Investors hope their property will appreciate.

113

stamp—a piece of paper placed on an envelope or package to show that the fee for mailing has been paid
  coin—a piece of metal with a certain value that is used as currency
  Independent nations always issue their own stamps and coins.
liquidity—ability to be converted (changed) into cash
  Investors are worried about the declining liquidity of their investment holdings.
ounce—measure of weight used in English-speaking countries, equivalent to approximately 28 grams
  The price of an ounce of gold has declined recently.

Supplementary Vocabulary

bull—an investor who counts on prices rising when he or she buys stocks
bear—an investor who counts on prices falling when he or she buys stocks

Vocabulary Practice

Select the answer that correctly completes each sentence.

1. I'm going to buy these stocks because they've been showing a good _____.
   a. earnings   b. growth rate   c. commission
2. How much was his _____ on that painting at the auction?
   a. fluctuation   b. bid   c. bargain
3. We can hardly pay for the necessities of life these days with this _____ inflation.
   a. declining   b. bullish   c. double-digit
4. Before acquiring more collectibles, Phil wants to check their _____.
   a. bargain   b. strategy   c. liquidity
5. Even dealers in gold coins and jewelry are being badly affected by the _____ market.
   a. bearish   b. recession   c. slowdown

INVESTMENTS (PART TWO)

Phil O'Brien has decided to follow Carol Levine's advice. He has made an appointment to see Jeff Hunter, a broker, to discuss how to invest the money that was bequeathed to him by his aunt. He's in Mr. Hunter's office now.

Mr. H.   Hello, Mr. O'Brien. It's good to meet you. Have a seat, please.
Mr. O'B. Thank you. As you may know, I wanted some advice about how to invest my aunt's money. I have almost no experience with investments and I feel I don't have enough knowledge or information to make intelligent choices. One of your clients, a Ms. Carol Levine, recommended that I see you.
Mr. H.   Well, I can understand your concern. There are many investment possibilities, and conditions fluctuate so much nowadays.
Mr. O'B. The first area I thought about was stocks. My wife and I have a few shares in utility companies already, so stocks are not completely strange to me.
Mr. H.   I should tell you that there are two ways to look at investing in stocks. First, there are long-term investments. You can put your money into stable companies with a relatively secure yield. Or, you can concentrate on buying stocks that promise a good, rapid growth rate and resell them at a profit.
Mr. O'B. Well, I guess the second option means that I'd have to watch the stock market pretty carefully. I know I don't have time for that.
Mr. H.   You're right. Your investment strategies would depend on whether you were facing a bullish or bearish market. You'd also have to consider factors in the economy such as a slowdown or a recession, double-digit inflation, interest rates, and other things that affect the companies you invest in.
Mr. O'B. I'd like to know what kind of stocks you've been recommending. Which sectors of the economy have been strong lately? What are the areas I ought to think about?
Mr. H.   Well, we've had some good results with high-yielding bank shares recently, and experts are predicting these will appreciate quickly in the near future. The data processing companies have been doing well and high technology stocks have also had high earnings.
Mr. O'B. I've read that the market has been pretty bearish lately. It must be a good time for bargain-hunters to invest.
Mr. H.   True, but bargain-hunters mustn't just buy stocks unless they make sure that the companies they invest in can maintain their growth through difficult times. Otherwise those investors may be faced with declining values.
Mr. O'B. What do you know about collectibles? I thought that they might offer some interesting possibilities for investment.
Mr. H.   You've got to be careful with collectibles nowadays. Works of art, stamps and coins are less in demand now and are proving rather

Mr. O'B.   difficult to sell. Prices are therefore dropping, and owners of collectibles are finding their liquidity limited.

Mr. O'B.   I can't believe it. It doesn't seem very long ago that dealers and auction-houses were making very big commissions. I remember some very high bids on paintings about a year ago.

Mr. H.   Yes, but that has changed. Even gold jewelry, which was in great demand because of the steadily rising price of gold, has become less popular as the value of an ounce of gold has fallen over the last six months.

Mr. O'B.   Well, you've given me some valuable information. Let me talk things over with my wife and I'll talk to you again next week.

Mr. H.   Good. Let's see if we can make some money for you!

Comprehension Check

A. State whether each statement is true or false based on the dialogue.

1. Phil O'Brien already owned some stock when he consulted Jeff Hunter.
2. Mr. O'Brien prefers the option that requires him to watch the stock market carefully.
3. His broker advises Mr. O'Brien that investment strategies depend on whether the stock market is bullish or bearish.
4. Mr. Hunter suggests that inflation and interest rates also affect the market.
5. Mr. Hunter is uncertain whether high-yielding bank shares will continue to appreciate.
6. Data processing and high technology stocks have had a good yield recently, according to Mr. Hunter.
7. Mr. O'Brien has read that prices have been rising in the market lately.
8. Mr. Hunter doesn't recommend investing in collectibles because they're no longer as easy to sell as they were before.
9. Paintings, unlike stamps and coins, have not lost any of their liquidity.
10. Her broker thinks that Mrs. O'Brien should sell her gold jewelry because of the steadily rising price of gold.

B. Answer the following questions orally.

1. What are the two ways to look at investing in stocks?
2. What are the factors that should be considered by someone who is developing his investment strategies?
3. What kinds of stocks have been doing well lately?
4. What do bargain-hunting investors who buy stocks in a bearish market have to be careful of?
5. What are collectibles? Why aren't they good investments nowadays?

C. Composition. Write a paragraph describing some of the investment strategies one can use in investing in the stock market. Refer to market conditions and other economic factors and mention specific types of investments.

Building Your Vocabulary

A. Matching. Find the words in the right-hand column that match the words closest in meaning in the left-hand column.

1. slowdown
2. choice
3. sale by bids
4. decreasing
5. inflation
6. rate of return on investment
7. commission
8. ability to be changed into cash

a. yield
b. process of rising prices
c. declining
d. liquidity
e. payment for broker's services
f. option
g. auction
h. a decrease in economic activity

B. Rewriting sentences. Rewrite each of the following sentences replacing the underlined word or words with the correct form of one of the new words of this lesson.

1. You should look into your <u>alternatives</u> before you invest in these stocks.
2. Mr. Halpern is an <u>investor who counts on prices falling in the stock market</u>.
3. This stock promises a very good <u>percentage of increase in value</u>.
4. The government is not dealing very successfully with this <u>period of temporary economic decline and unemployment</u>.
5. We're hoping our shares in the data processing company will give us <u>a high income</u>.
6. Cathy Caruso is <u>an investor who buys stocks when prices rise</u>.
7. The broker told me my <u>stamps and coins</u> would be quite difficult to sell right now.
8. He's selling these works of art now because he's afraid their <u>ability to be converted into cash</u> will be decreasing.

PRESENTATION

Modals

I, You, He, She, We, They { should, must, ought to, may, might, can, could } consider other investment strategies.

$\left.\begin{array}{l}\text{I}\\ \text{You}\\ \text{He}\\ \text{She}\\ \text{We}\\ \text{They}\end{array}\right\} \left\{\begin{array}{ll}\text{should not} & \text{(shouldn't)}\\ \text{must not} & \text{(mustn't)}\\ \text{ought not} & (* \quad)\\ \text{may not} & (* \quad)\\ \text{might not} & \text{(might not)}\\ \text{cannot} & \text{(can't)}\\ \text{could not} & \text{(couldn't)}\end{array}\right\}$ invest in collectibles now.

$\left.\begin{array}{l}\text{Should}\\ \text{Must}\\ \text{Ought}\\ \text{May}\\ \text{Might}\\ \text{Can}\\ \text{Could}\end{array}\right\} \left\{\begin{array}{l}\text{I}\\ \text{you}\\ \text{he}\\ \text{she}\\ \text{we}\\ \text{they}\end{array}\right\}$ study the stock market carefully?

$\left.\begin{array}{ll}\text{Shouldn't I} & \text{(Should I not)}\\ \text{Mustn't I} & \text{(Must I not)}\\ \text{Mightn't I} & \text{(Might I not)}\\ \text{Can't I} & \text{(Can I not)}\\ \text{Couldn't I} & \text{(Could I not)}\end{array}\right\}$ see a broker?

Some special meanings of the modals:

We have to earn more. = We *must* earn more.
                    but
We don't have to earn more. ≠ We *mustn't* earn more.
We don't have to earn more. = It isn't necessary for us to earn more.
We *mustn't* earn more. = It is forbidden for us to earn more.
We *must* earn more. = We have to earn more. or
                          It would seem that we earned more.
May I go? = Do I have permission to go?
Can I go? = Do I have permission to go? or
              Am I able to go?
This stock *may* appreciate. = This stock *might* appreciate.
We *should* study the market. = We *ought to* study the market.
Can I go? = *Could* I go? (asks permission)

*Seldom contracted in American English.

Structure Practice

A. As an investor in the stock market you go to your broker for advice. Ask him what you should do by transforming each of the following statements into questions. Use the modal *should*.

Model: I invest money now.
→ Should I invest money now?

1. I consider several options.
2. My wife and I invest in stocks with a pretty secure yield.
3. I buy stocks in a bearish market.
4. I take into account double-digit inflation.
5. We invest in data processing companies.
6. I concentrate on high technology stocks.
7. I look for bargains in the market.
8. We buy collectibles.

B. Now take the role of a broker and answer the questions that the client asks in exercise A using the modal *ought to*.

Model: "Should I invest money now?"
"Yes, you ought to invest money now."

C. Your broker wants to check with you before she takes steps to improve your stock portfolio. She asks you questions using *can* and you respond with *may* in your replies.

Model: "Can I sell 20% of your shares in the electric company?"
"Yes, you may sell 20% of those shares."

1. Can I buy some high-yielding bank shares for you?
2. Can I suggest some new investment strategies to you?
3. Can I use a part of your earnings to buy high technology stocks?
4. Can I also invest some of your earnings in data processing companies?
5. Can I speculate for you on some stocks that promise a rapid growth rate?
6. Can I look into collectibles for you?

D. Expand each of the following sentences with *may*, as in the model. *May* expresses conjecture here (that is, a guess).

Model: He wants to consider his options.
→ He may want to consider his options.

1. They wait until interest rates fall.
2. I watch the stock market very carefully.
3. We're facing a bullish market now.
4. Ms. Chen needs some advice on investing.
5. The brokers recommend high technology stocks to you.
6. There are many bargain-hunters in the market.
7. Paintings prove difficult to sell.
8. Bank shares offer some good possibilities.

E. Repeat exercise D, this time expanding each sentence with *might*. *Might* also expresses conjecture.

   Model: He wants to consider his options.
   → He might want to consider his options.

F. Your wife is curious about your friend's dealings in the stock market. She asks you questions about Ned but discovers that you are not too sure about what happened. Use *might have* + past participle in your answer to express conjecture about what happened in the past.

   Model: "Did Ned earn a lot of money?"
   "I'm not sure. He might have earned a lot of money."
   1. Did Ned buy a lot of stocks?
   2. Did he consult a brokerage firm?
   3. Did he study the stock market carefully?
   4. Did Ned invest in stocks with a relatively secure yield?
   5. Did he have shares in utility companies?
   6. Did Ned look into collectibles?
   7. Did he check the current liquidity of works of art?
   8. Did he consider economic factors such as inflation?

G. Repeat exercise F, this time answering your wife's questions with *may* + past participle to express conjecture about past events.

   Model: "Did Ned earn money?"
   "I'm not sure. He may have earned money."

H. You are a broker. Your client, Millicent Cooper, comes to you for advice about her stocks. To each question she asks about what she should do, respond with an answer telling her what she *must* do in her best interest.

   Model: "Should I wait to invest until the market is bullish?"
   "Yes, you must wait until the market is bullish."
   1. Should I consider some new plans of action?
   2. Should I find some other options for investing?
   3. Should I sell some stocks during this recession?
   4. Should I look for some bargain stocks?
   5. Should I buy the bank shares you recommended?
   6. Should I dispose of these stocks with declining values?
   7. Should I put some of my money into high technology stocks?
   8. Should I concentrate on stocks that promise a rapid growth rate?

I. Answer each of the following questions with a statement that uses *must* to express probability. Use the cues in parentheses in your answers.

   Model: "What time does the stock exchange open?" (9 A.M.)
   "I don't know. It must open at 9 A.M."
   1. How much money are they losing with those stocks? (thousands of dollars)
   2. When does the board meeting start? (around 10:30)

3. What's the rate of inflation now? (about 12%)
4. How many companies do you own stock in? (19 or 20)
5. Where is Mr. Chan now? (with a client)
6. How old is that painting? (250 years old)
7. Who is Jean Summer? (the new broker)
8. Which of these stocks has the highest growth rate? (the data processing stocks)

J. Rewrite each of the following statements in the negative. Use contractions whenever you can correctly do so.

Model: They should buy shares in this company.
→ They shouldn't buy shares in this company.

1. We ought to follow our old investment strategies.
2. He should have kept only common stock.
3. You must sell your sculpture collection.
4. Barbara might have gone to a brokerage firm.
5. I may try to find a bargain.
6. Their investment strategies must depend only on falling prices.
7. You ought to have sold your securities.
8. The slowdown should be continuing.

Building Sentences

A. Select elements from columns **A, B, C** and **D** to form at least ten affirmative sentences with modals. Add words as needed so that the sentences you write make sense.

A	B	C	D
You	should	be	strategies
We	may	sell	growth rate
Phil O'Brien	ought to	consider	options
The property	might	invest (in)	yield
I	must	appreciate	collectibles
These stocks	can	buy	declining value
The stock market	could	have	inflation
The dealer		look into	slowdown
Bargain-hunters		find	bullish
		need	data processing
		show	auction
		make	bearish
		want	high technology
		recommend	bids
		think about	liquidity
			commission

Investments (Part II) **121**

B. Rearrange the elements of each group to form a sentence containing a modal. You may add words if necessary.
1. options/ought to/other/you/consider
2. we/stocks/invest in/high technology/should
3. a/face/investors/may/market/bearish
4. might/coins/limited/she/find/liquidity/the
5. concentrate on/other/he/possibilities/must/investment
6. during/not/buy/shares/recession/should/I/the/more
7. may/a/gold/Carol/to/sell/her/jewelry/dealer
8. count on/prices/these/rising/investors/might

C. Complete each of the following sentences by selecting either *a* or *b*.
1. You _____ to watch the stock market carefully.
   a. ought   b. should
2. They _____ not invest in a bullish market.
   a. should   b. mightn't
3. Those stocks _____ shown a good growth rate.
   a. may   b. must have
4. "Should I try to sell my coin collection?"
   "Yes, you really _____ sell it."
   a. might have   b. ought to
5. "Did Tom consider other economic factors before he bought those shares?"
   "I'm not sure. He _____."
   a. might have   b. may
6. She _____ wait until the inflation rate drops.
   a. may   b. must have
7. "Can I buy some data processing stocks for your portfolio?"
   "No, you _____."
   a. should   b. may not
8. These bids are too high. We _____ let them go higher.
   a. mustn't   b. might
9. "You must continue that strategy."
   "You're right. I _____."
   a. might   b. should
10. These works of art _____ be worth half a million dollars.
    a. ought   b. must

BANKING CONVERSATIONS

A client has come to your brokerage firm for advice about his investments. Explain to him the investment strategies he might want to follow, the nature of the stock market he's facing right now, the economic factors that should influence his decision to buy or sell stocks, and the kinds of stocks that represent a good investment and those that you would not recommend.

READING PLUS

Now that you have completed another lesson on investments, you can read the following advertisement for *High Technology Growth Stocks*, an investment advisory service. The subscription is for the monthly guide (publication). First, study the following words and phrases.

issue—an edition of a newspaper or a magazine
back issue—an old issue of a newspaper or a magazine
range—extent, span, difference
statistical—pertaining to statistics, the science of quantitative data
delisted—taken off a list
high technology oriented—concentrating on or interested in high technology companies
emerging—new, coming into the market unexpectedly
subscription—an agreement to receive a certain number of issues of a magazine after paying a certain price; e.g., a two-year subscription
enclosed—placed in an envelope
(three-month) trial—a (three-month) test to see if a product is satisfactory
computer peripherals—equipment added to a computer that widens the range of its functions
CAD/CAM—Computer-aided design/computer-aided manufacture—refers to products designed and manufactured by computer systems

Now read the advertisement and answer the questions about it.

High Technology Growth Stocks

High Technology Growth Stocks is a new monthly investment advisory service which concentrates on identifying attractive fast-growing high technology companies with sales typically in the $5 million to $100 million range.

Each issue concentrates on a fast-growth high technology market and contains the following major sections: (1) discussion of the market, (2) selected stock of the month from the given market, (3) other recommended companies serving that market, (4) selected high technology new issue of the month, (5) other attractive high technology new issues, (6) a calendar of all high technology new issues for the month, (7) company news on previous and still recommended high technology stocks and (8) a master list with statistical data on all recommended high technology stocks.

Previous recommendations are followed until delisted. Each recommendation includes an easily understood description of the products/services offered by the company.

The editor has had extensive experience in analyzing high technology-oriented markets and a high success rate in identifying/selecting emerging fast-growing high technology companies.

FW9-15

Yes, I am interested in emerging fast-growing high technology growth stocks.

☐ Please enter my subscription to High Technology Growth Stocks for 1 year. Enclosed is $95.

☐ Please enter my subscription for a 3 month trial. Enclosed is $30.

☐ Please send me back issues covering the following markets:
  ☐ Data Communications
  ☐ Computers
  ☐ Computer Peripherals
  ☐ Medical Equipment/Supplies
  ☐ CAD/CAM
  ☐ Office Automation

☐ Enclosed is $10 for each back issue checked.

High Technology Growth Stocks
402 Border Road
Concord, MA 01742

Name _____

Address _____

City _____

State _____ Zip _____

Reprinted from the September 15, 1981 issue of *Financial World* by permission of the publisher, © 1981.

Questions

1. How often is *High Technology Growth Stocks* published?
2. What does *High Technology Growth Stocks* concentrate on?
3. What is the range of sales in these high technology companies?
4. What are the major sections in the publication?
5. What does the master list in (8) show?
6. What does each recommendation include?
7. What do you know about the editor of the publication from this advertisement?
8. What is the price of a one-year subscription to *High Technology Growth Stocks*?
9. *What does it cost to try High Technology Growth Stocks* for three months?
10. How much does each back issue cost?
11. Which markets can you find out about in back issues?
12. Are you billed by mail for the subscription and back issues?

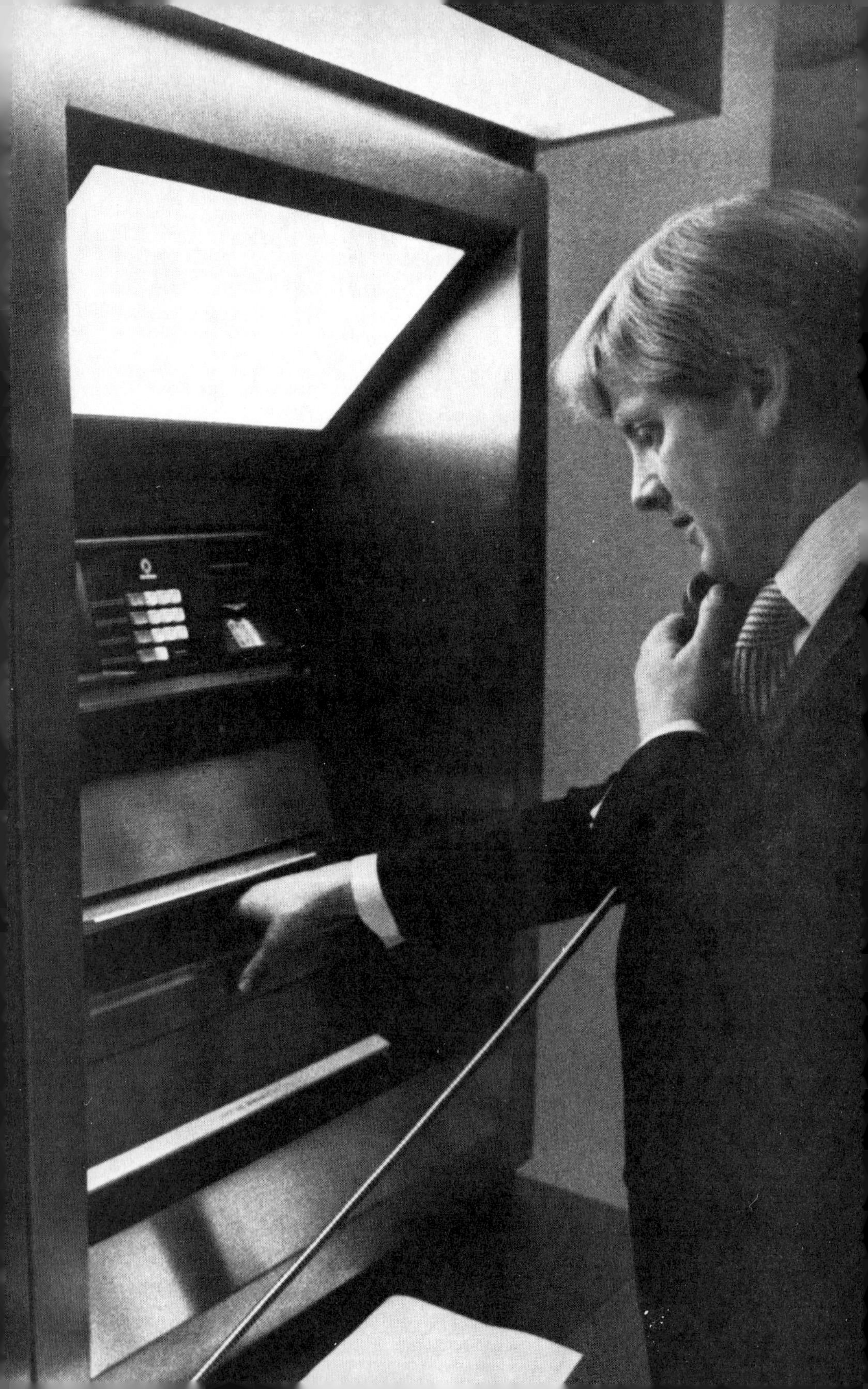

LESSON 13

ELECTRONIC BANKING

VOCABULARY

to retire—to stop working, leave one's job because of age
technology—the use of scientific advances in practical ways
device—a machine
electronic funds transfer—the use of electronic devices to record money moved from one account to another
electronically—using computers or other electric equipment
instant retrieval—immediate recovery of information
automatic teller machine—an electronic device that performs simple bank operations such as deposits and withdrawals
code number—a number that a bank customer uses to work the automatic teller
Social Security—a system of government pensions for retired persons (in the U.S.)
far-reaching—having a great and deep effect
storage—keeping in a safe place for future use
mailing—sending through the postal system
to reduce—to lower, lessen, make less or fewer, make smaller
to itemize—to make a list of the items or details of something
term—word or phrase
check truncation—an electronic system used by banks to reduce the work and cost of processing checks
payor—the person who pays, the person who writes the check

Expansion

procedure—official way of doing something
There are special procedures for opening and closing accounts.
entry—an item or transaction recorded on paper or by an electronic device
Each deposit or withdrawal means a new entry in the customer's passbook.
wage—money that an employer pays to a worker for his or her work
Wages are usually figured on a daily or hourly basis.
salary—payment for work made at regular intervals such as weekly or monthly
He's looking for a job with a high salary.

bill—note or letter demanding payment for goods or services
   I pay my bills on the first of every month.
to process—to perform the necessary steps or operations to do something
   We will try to process your application as quickly as possible.
handling costs—the expense caused by processing or managing
   Handling costs for processing checks are high.
check safekeeping—a procedure for the electronic storage of checks
microfilm—a film on which records are photographed in reduced size
   Banks use microfilm in check safekeeping.
to clear—said of a check when it is collected and paid
check-clearing process—the steps necessary for a check to clear
   It takes one week for a check drawn on a local bank to clear.

Vocabulary Practice

Select the answer that correctly completes each sentence.

1. You can't withdraw the money until the check _____.
   a. clears   b. reduces   c. retires
2. The last _____ recorded in the passbook is a deposit on September 28.
   a. device   b. term   c. entry
3. The computers provide _____ of bank transactions.
   a. technology   b. instant retrieval   c. check truncation
4. I hope the credit department _____ my loan application quickly.
   a. processes   b. projects   c. itemizes
5. All these changes in banking procedures are _____.
   a. check safekeeping   b. far-reaching   c. handling

ELECTRONIC BANKING

Marta Conway, 65 years old, is retiring from her job as a teller after 40 years of service at the Bridgewater Savings Bank. She's having lunch with Penny Nichols, a young teller who has just started working at the bank.

Penny   Marta, you must know this bank better than anyone. I'll bet banking has changed a lot since you started working here.

Marta   You're so right, Penny. I've seen many changes in banking procedures over the last 40 years. Sometimes it seems that the job I do now is nothing like the job I did when I began my work here.

Penny   In what aspect of your job have you seen the greatest changes?

Marta   That's easy to answer. I think the most striking changes in banking over the 40 years that I've been here have come from technology. All the advances in electronic banking have made being a teller very different now from when I was a young woman.

Penny   That's true. The other new tellers and I take things like computers for granted, but if I think about it, they haven't been around all that long.

Marta   That's right. I can still remember when we wrote each new entry in a customer's passbook by hand. The computers now do all that at the press of a button.

Penny   What do you think about electronic funds transfer? Even for us younger employees, it's a really new concept.

Marta   Well, Penny, if someone had told me 40 years ago that people would be able to do their banking without paper, I wouldn't have believed it.

Penny   I know. And here is a system where a customer's transactions, such as deposits and withdrawals, are recorded electronically and then stored in a computer's memory. When you have to check the records, the computer provides instant retrieval.

Marta   Those automatic teller machines have proved to be very useful, especially for our customers. Now they have access to their accounts at any time of day or night, 365 days a year. Since these devices are on the outside walls of banks, customers can use their plastic cards and code numbers to deposit, withdraw, or transfer money from one account to another even when the bank is closed.

Penny   These electronic funds transfer devices do save us a lot of paperwork. And think how much time automatic deposit saves us!

Marta   Exactly. Now, not only Social Security benefits but also wages, salaries and stock dividends can be automatically deposited into an account. The payor doesn't even have to write a check! Using EFT procedures, he notifies the bank electronically to transfer the appropriate sum from his account to the payee's account. And the two accounts don't even have to be at the same bank!

Penny   And EFT is really just beginning. When combined with the telephone, the changes in banking are really far-reaching. You know, I've started paying some of my bills by phone. I just call the bank and authorize

	them to transfer the money I owe from any account to the account of the electric company, gas company, or phone company automatically. That way, I take care of my bills without writing checks.
Marta	Writing fewer checks means, of course, more time saved for the bank's customers, but it also has advantages for the banks. I remember a course I took in banking a few years ago. We were told that in 1979, over 30 billion checks were written in the United States. Incredible! And the professor said that the figure was expected to rise to 50 billion by 1985. Now it costs banks about 16 cents to process each check and these handling costs are passed on to the customers.
Penny	Sure. Storage and mailing of checks are expensive. The new technology really promises to cut costs there. Have you heard about check safekeeping?
Marta	Yes, it's a system where the bank stores the customer's checks on microfilm rather than returning them to him or her every month. The monthly statement would itemize all the checks written by the customer. The microfilm storage would provide our customers with a permanent record of their checks. Think of the savings in space alone.
Penny	Another system I've heard about recently is check truncation. Many people confuse it with check safekeeping, and there are some similarities. Both procedures are designed to reduce the amount of paperwork for banks. Check safekeeping operates between the bank and its customers. Check truncation operates among banks. You know how slow our current check-clearing procedures are.
Marta	Of course I do. In order for a check to clear, it must be presented to the bank where the payor's account is maintained, even if the bank is a thousand miles away. That's why it sometimes takes two weeks for a check to clear. It would be wonderful if the check-clearing process could be speeded up.
Penny	That's what check truncation is designed to do. With this new electronic procedure the check is kept at the bank where it is presented. That bank sends an electronic message to the bank that the check is drawn against. The bank where the payor has his account can than make the payment electronically. And the expense and delay of mailing the check itself are thereby avoided.
Marta	That's marvelous. And I'm sure this is only the beginning of the electronic revolution in banking. If you remain in banking, Penny, you'll see some very exciting changes in the future!

Comprehension Check

A. State whether each sentence is true or false based on the reading.

1. Marta Conway has lost her job to an automatic teller machine.
2. Electronic banking reduces the amount of paperwork for tellers.
3. Automatic teller machines operate during banking hours only.

4. Customers must have code numbers to operate the automatic teller machines.
5. Electronic funds transfer devices make it possible for payors to pay bills without writing checks.
6. The customers' checks are stored on microfilm in the system known as check safekeeping.
7. Check truncation is designed to speed up the check-clearing process.
8. Check truncation eliminate the delay and expense of mailing checks from one bank to another.

B. Answer the following questions orally.

1. How is technology changing banking procedures?
2. How have tellers been affected by electronic banking?
3. How do automatic teller machines benefit customers? How do they operate?
4. In the electronic funds transfer procedure, what funds can be deposited and how are they deposited?
5. How do check safekeeping and check truncation differ?

C. **Composition.** Write a paragraph describing some of the new features of electronic banking and explain the advantages they offer to banks and bank customers.

Building Your Vocabulary

A. **Matching.** Find the words in the right-hand column that are closest in meaning to the words in the left-hand column.

1. person who writes a check
2. using computers
3. keeping in a safe place
4. bill
5. processing expenses
6. itemize
7. code number
8. salary
9. stop working
10. term

a. figure used to work an automatic teller
b. storage
c. word
d. payment for work
e. retire
f. note demanding payment
g. payor
h. handling costs
i. electronically
j. make a list

B. **Rewriting sentences.** Rewrite each of the following sentences replacing the underlined word or words with the correct form of one of the new words of this lesson.

Model: This new computer is such a useful <u>machine</u>.
→ This new computer is such a useful device.

1. Banking today is so much easier now that <u>electronic devices to record transactions</u> are used.
2. The boss pays his workers <u>money</u> each week.

3. When we retire we'll receive money from <u>the government pensions program</u>.
4. Technology has greatly <u>lessened</u> the teller's paperwork.
5. The customers' checks are stored on microfilm in <u>this procedure of electronic check storage</u>.
6. The teller can't read the signature of the <u>person who wrote the check</u>.
7. Check-clearing procedures are made easier because of <u>this electronic check processing system</u>.
8. The bank <u>makes a list of</u> all the checks that I write each month on my monthly statement.

PRESENTATION

A. Conditional

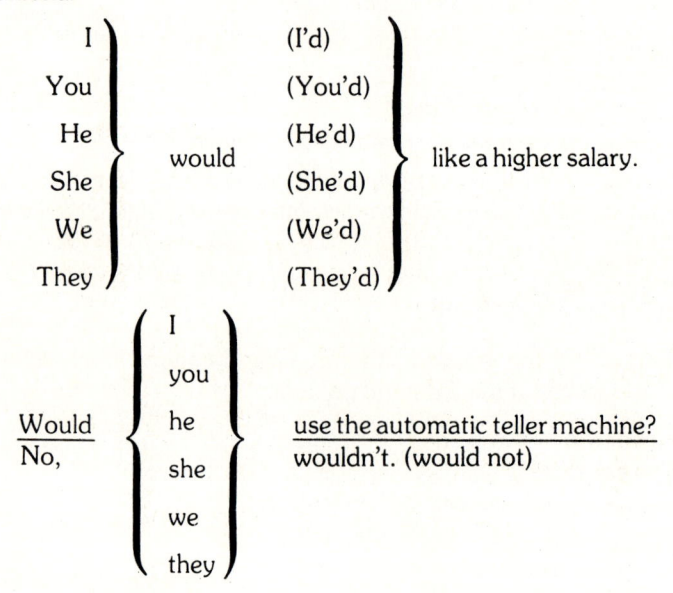

$$\left.\begin{array}{l}\text{I}\\ \text{You}\\ \text{He}\\ \text{She}\\ \text{We}\\ \text{They}\end{array}\right\} \text{would} \left.\begin{array}{l}\text{(I'd)}\\ \text{(You'd)}\\ \text{(He'd)}\\ \text{(She'd)}\\ \text{(We'd)}\\ \text{(They'd)}\end{array}\right\} \text{like a higher salary.}$$

$$\begin{array}{l}\underline{\text{Would}}\\ \underline{\text{No,}}\end{array} \left\{\begin{array}{l}\text{I}\\ \text{you}\\ \text{he}\\ \text{she}\\ \text{we}\\ \text{they}\end{array}\right\} \begin{array}{l}\underline{\text{use the automatic teller machine?}}\\ \text{wouldn't. (would not)}\end{array}$$

B. Conditional sentences

1. If the boss pays higher wages, she'll have better workers.

2. If Bob retires this year, he'll have nothing to keep him busy.

3. The bank would save time and money if it used electronic devices.
   (But it doesn't use them.)

4. You'd have accurate records if you itemized everything.
   (But you don't itemize everything.)

5. If I had reduced my costs, my profits would have been higher.
   (But I didn't reduce my costs so my profits weren't higher.)

6. We'd have purchased a house if we had gotten a mortgage.
   (But we didn't get a mortgage so we didn't purchase a house.)

Structure Practice

A. As president of the bank, you are trying to convince your board of directors that introducing electronic devices would make your bank run more efficiently. Explain what benefits you would get by changing each of the following present tense sentences to sentences with a verb in the conditional.

> Model: We save money on mailing costs.
> → We'd save money on mailing costs.

1. The tellers have less paperwork.
2. Computers make entries in customers' passbooks.
3. Each transaction is recorded electronically.
4. The computer provides instant retrieval.
5. With the automatic teller machines, the customers have access to their accounts 24 hours a day.
6. The electronic funds transfer devices make it possible for funds to be deposited automatically.
7. We store the customers' checks on microfilm in check safekeeping.
8. Check truncation speeds up the check-clearing process.
9. We reduce handling costs.
10. We pass on savings to our customers.

B. You and the other bank employees are discussing what changes there would be in your work if the bank introduced electronic devices. Change each of the following sentences from the present to the conditional.

> Model: Technology brings many changes to banking.
> → Technology would bring many changes to banking.

1. The tellers don't write entries in passbooks by hand anymore.
2. All transactions are recorded electronically.
3. I check the records in the computer.
4. We lose our jobs to the automatic teller machines.
5. Lois saves paperwork.
6. Steven loses his job.
7. We don't receive a raise in salary.
8. We need less space with the storage of records on microfilm.
9. You don't wait long for checks to clear.
10. We see far-reaching changes in banking.

C. Restate each of the following sentences changing *can* to *could* in the *if*-clause and the verb from future to conditional in the independent clause.

> Model: If I can go to the bank, I'll take you.
> → If I could go to the bank, I'd take you.

1. If we can afford the electronic device, we'll buy it.
2. If Mr. Adams can retire this year, he'll move to California.
3. If you can remember your code number, you'll be able to use the automatic teller.
4. If they can speed up the process, I'll get my loan by December.

5. She won't be able to pay the bill if she can't find it.
6. If I can itemize the entries, I'll have very organized records.
7. The bank will reduce its costs if it can introduce technological advances.
8. Bank procedures will take less time if the employees can operate the new machines.

D. Complete each of the following sentences about modern technology in banking with an appropriate conditional clause.

Model: If the bank used check truncation, . . .
→ If the bank used check truncation, payments would be made electronically. or
→ If the bank used check truncation, checks would clear more rapidly.

1. If the tellers used computers, . . .
2. If there were automatic teller machines, . . .
3. If the bank introduced electronic funds transfer procedures, . . .
4. If the EFT system were combined with the telephone, . . .
5. If the bank had increased handling costs, . . .
6. If check safekeeping were instituted in banks, . . .
7. If the customer's checks were stored on microfilm, . . .
8. If all banks participated in the electronic revolution, . . .

E. Answer the following questions negatively, as in the model.

Model: "Would you like to see a broker?"
"No, I wouldn't."

1. Would they use electronic funds transfer procedures?
2. Would she retire this year?
3. Would that employer pay higher wages?
4. Would the payor have to wait for the check to clear?
5. Would you be able to tell me what this term means?
6. Would I reduce my paperwork?
7. Would we know how to operate the automatic teller machines?
8. Would the deposits be recorded electronically?

F. Restate each of the following sentences in the past, as in the model.

Model: I'd invest in stocks if I had the funds.
→ I would have invested in stocks if I had had the funds.

1. He'd reduce his paperwork if he had a computer.
2. They'd retire if they could get Social Security.
3. Angela would use the automatic teller machine if she could find her plastic card.
4. We'd pay our bills by phone if our bank instituted those electronic systems.
5. I wouldn't be short of money each month if I earned a higher salary.
6. You'd spend the money in the trust fund if you needed it.

G. Answer each of the following questions with an appropriate response in the conditional.

> Model: "What would you do if you needed a loan?"
> "I'd apply for one."
> "What would you have done if you had needed a loan?"
> "I would have applied for one."

1. What would you do if you lost your job?
2. What would you have done if you had lost your checkbook?
3. What would you do if the bank you worked in introduced all new electronic devices?
4. What would you have done if the computer had broken down?
5. What would you do if you forgot your code number for the ATM?
6. What would you have done if your Social Security benefits hadn't been deposited automatically into your account?

Building Sentences

A. Select elements from columns **A**, **B** and **C** to form at least ten affirmative and negative sentences in the conditional. Add any necessary words.

A	B	C
Ms. Conway	introduce	paperwork
We	pay	electronic funds transfer
They	retire	computers
I	explain	bills
The bank	purchase	salary
You	like	procedures
The board of directors	itemize	automatic teller machines
The payor	write	entries
The employees	receive	check-clearing process
Some tellers	speed up	checks
	use	technology
		code numbers
		Social Security
		electronic device

B. Complete each of the following sentences by selecting the correct word for the blank space.

1. We _____ like to earn a higher salary.
   a. could   b. would
2. The tellers _____ save paperwork if they used computers.
   a. could   b. can

Electronic Banking

3. I would use the automatic teller machine if I _____ remember my code number.
   a. would   b. could
4. _____ you like to speed up these procedures?
   a. Wouldn't   b. Couldn't
5. If I _____ bought an electronic device, I would have reduced my costs.
   a. had   b. could
6. She _____ understand why the check hadn't cleared.
   a. couldn't   b. hasn't
7. _____ I see my itemized statement of deposits and withdrawals, please?
   a. Would   b. Could
8. Mr. Nicholas would have retired from his job if he _____ been 65 years old.
   a. would   b. had

C. Use the elements in each string to form a sentence in the conditional. Add words as necessary.

Model: you/save/time/electronic devices
→ You would save time with electronic devices.
1. far-reaching/changes/come/technology
2. customer's/checks/stored/microfilm
3. check truncation/operate/banks
4. electronic devices/speed up/check-clearing procedures
5. bank/send/electronic message/bank
6. they/institute/check safekeeping
7. wages/deposited/automatically/account
8. bank/transfer/funds/payee's/account
9. transactions/recorded/electronically
10. teller/write/entry/passbook

BANKING CONVERSATIONS

A. A new teller in your bank would like to know about the electronic devices and procedures currently in use. Since you have been a teller for several years and are well acquainted with them, you can explain these operations to him. Tell him about the following:
   a. electronic funds transfer
   b. check safekeeping
   c. check truncation
   d. instant retrieval

B. You are head of the board of directors of a bank. You have suggested instituting automatic teller machines in the bank and the other directors have asked you for information about them. Explain to them why you believe the ATMs are important for the bank and its customers and describe the procedures in the operation of these machines.

READING PLUS

Now that you have studied several aspects of electronic banking you can examine the workings of an automatic teller machine, known as "Iris." This ATM is found at the Brookline Savings Bank. Before you read about "Iris," study the following words and phrases.

station—(here) teller's window
home free—(baseball term) safe, successfully finished
portion—part
to validate—to make legal or official
validator—part of the ATM that validates receipts
chute—slot or opening that the envelope is put into
downright—quite, very, really
depository—(here) machine for deposits
face up—front side facing upward
to retain—to keep

After you learn the meanings of the words in the list above, study the information on "Iris" and answer the questions that follow.

Electronic Banking

IRIS

IRIS IS FAST-
6 SECONDS FAST

YOUR DEPOSIT TRANSACTION IS HANDLED IN JUST 6 SECONDS EVEN IF YOU DEPOSIT TO 10 DIFFERENT ACCOUNTS. THE ENTIRE TRANSACTION STILL TAKES JUST 6 SECONDS NOT ONLY THAT BUT THERE ARE NO LINES AT THIS "TELLERS" STATION.

WHEN YOU ARE IN A HURRY THINK "IRIS"-SHE'LL GET YOU OUT AND ON YOUR WAY.

IRIS IS UNCOMPLICATED-

IF YOU CAN FILL OUT A DEPOSIT SLIP AND PLACE IT IN AN ENVELOPE, YOU'RE PRACTICALLY HOME FREE.

AFTER YOU HAVE DONE THIS, AND NOTED YOUR TRANSACTION ON THE ENVELOPE YOU TEAR OFF THE RECEIPT PORTION.

THE RECEIPT IS PLACED IN THE VALIDATOR AND THE ENVELOPE IN THE DEPOSIT CHUTE.

INSTANTANEOUSLY YOUR DEPOSIT IS SAFELY LOCKED AWAY AND YOU HAVE A STAMPED VALIDATED RECEIPT FOR YOUR RECORDS. "IRIS" IS NOT JUST UNCOMPLICATED- SHE'S DOWNRIGHT SIMPLE.

"IRIS" WAS DESIGNED FOR YOU-

"IRIS" IS AN INSTALLED SERVICE TRULY DESIGNED FOR THE BENEFIT OF THE DEPOSITOR.

WE DON'T WANT TO SEE YOU STANDING IN LONG LINES ANY MORE THAN YOU DO.

SINGLE AND MULTIPLE DEPOSITS OR PAYMENTS CAN BE ACCOMMODATED IN JUST 6 SECONDS WHICH ALLOWS YOU TO GO ON YOUR WAY WITHOUT INCONVENIENCE.

"IRIS" IS SECURE AND PROVIDES YOU WITH A VALIDATED RECEIPT.

LUNCH HOURS SHOULD NOT BE SPENT STANDING IN LINE AT A BANK — EVEN OURS — TO PREVENT THIS WE HAVE INSTALLED "IRIS" — JUST FOR YOU.

"As Simple as A-B-C"

FOR A CUSTOMER TO MAKE A DEPOSIT IN OUR NEW, QUICK AND AUTOMATED BANK DEPOSITORY.

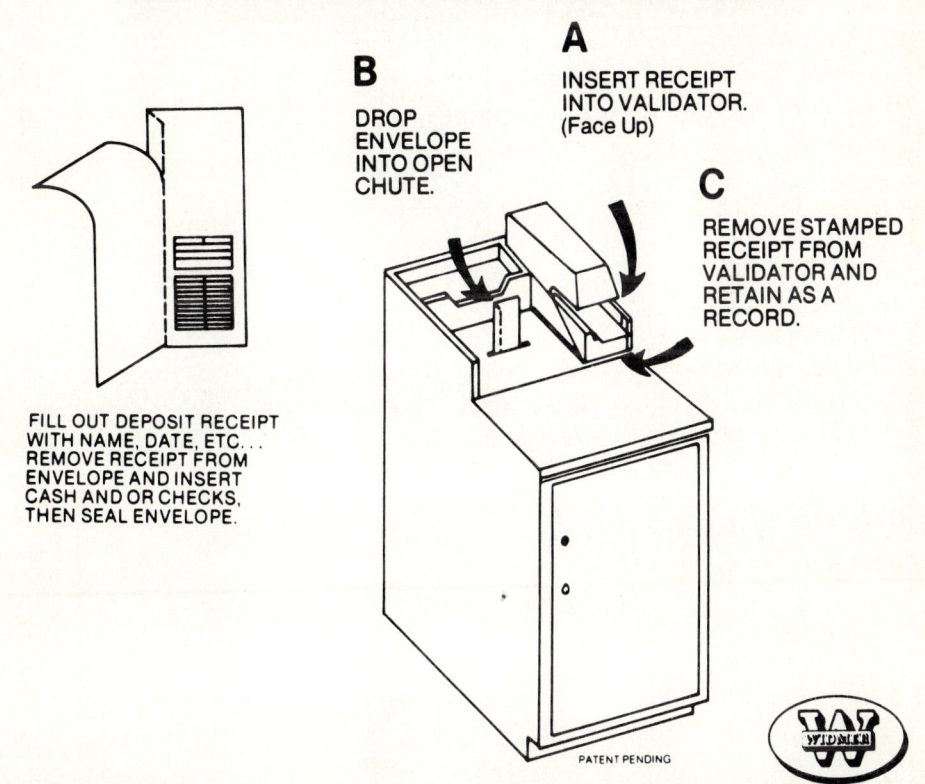

A INSERT RECEIPT INTO VALIDATOR. (Face Up)

B DROP ENVELOPE INTO OPEN CHUTE.

C REMOVE STAMPED RECEIPT FROM VALIDATOR AND RETAIN AS A RECORD.

FILL OUT DEPOSIT RECEIPT WITH NAME, DATE, ETC... REMOVE RECEIPT FROM ENVELOPE AND INSERT CASH AND OR CHECKS, THEN SEAL ENVELOPE.

PATENT PENDING

Reprinted by permission of the Brookline Savings Bank, Brookline, Massachusetts, U.S.A.

Questions

1. How long does a deposit transaction take?
2. Do you have to wait in line?
3. What procedures must you follow to make a deposit?
4. Where do you place the receipt?
5. Where do you place the envelope?
6. What do you put into the envelope?
7. What record do you have of your transaction?
8. How is the receipt inserted into the validator?
9. What are the benefits to the depositor in using "Iris"?
10. Why would you use an ATM rather than go to the teller inside the bank?

Electronic Banking

FOREIGN CURRENCY

CURRENCY	BUY	SELL
CANADIAN	.8204	.8455
ITALIAN LIRA	.000783	.0009
FRENCH FRANCS	.1655	.1861
SWISS FRANCS	.4830	.5025
DEUTSCHE MARKS	.4095	.4280
STERLING PDS.	1.90	1.99
JAPANESE YEN	.00432	.00455
SPANISH PESETAS	.0094	.0117
MEXICAN PESOS	.038	.045
DUTCH GUILDERS	.3675	.3871
GREEK DRACHMAS	.0150	.0196
SHEKELS	.0857	.0883

RATES SUBJECT TO CHANGE

LESSON 14

DEVALUATION

VOCABULARY

realignment—adjustment, bringing back into agreement
to realign—to adjust, to bring into agreement
European Monetary System—agreement among European nations that limits the margin of fluctuation in exchange rates
foreign trade—buying and selling of one country's products in foreign countries
multinational corporation—a company that produces its goods in more than one country
revaluation—a change in the value of a currency
speculative pressure—the influence of speculators in currency on the exchange rates
to trigger—to start, begin, set off, put into motion
value—worth, price; (here) amount of a foreign currency that the national currency will bring
foreign exchange markets—markets where sellers agree to supply currencies to buyers at a specified date in the future for a fixed price
to support—to strengthen, make stronger
to float—to allow the value of a currency to be determined by supply and demand (said of currency)
to bolster—to support
to restrict—to limit, control
monetary expansion—increase in the money supply
unemployment—lack or shortage of jobs for people who want to work
exports—goods and services that are produced in one country and that are sold abroad (in a foreign country)
imports—foreign goods and services brought to and sold in a country

Expansion

balance of trade—the value of a nation's exports compared to the value of its imports
Countries that import more than they export are said to have a negative balance of trade.

reserves—gold and foreign currency held by a country and used to repay debts
 The U.S. dollar has been a traditional reserve currency.
record—highest or lowest level
 Inflation rates have reached a new record low this month.
flight of capital—excessive investment of money in foreign countries
 High interest rates in the U.S. have triggered a flight of capital from Latin America.
public sector—that part of the economy that consists of government (national, state and provincial, and local) plus public corporations
 The public sector is increasing in most Western countries.
differential—difference between two variable values
 The differential in French and German interest rates has risen.
energy—fuel such as oil or coal
 The high cost of energy has caused inflation and balance of trade deficits in the industrialized nations.

Supplementary Vocabulary

to export—to sell abroad the goods and services produced in a country
to import—to bring foreign goods and services to a country for sale

Vocabulary Practice

Select the answer that correctly completes each sentence.

1. Inflation rates reached a _____ high in September.
   a. reserve   b. expansion   c. record
2. Frenchmen will be paying more for goods _____ from Holland and Germany.
   a. triggered   b. imported   c. realigned
3. The government feels that there has been too much monetary expansion, so they're trying to _____ it.
   a. restrict   b. bolster   c. export
4. The European Monetary System advises that currencies not be allowed to _____.
   a. increase   b. float   c. support
5. There has been a sudden _____ from the country.
   a. balance of trade   b. flight of capital   c. public sector
6. The country enjoyed a higher _____ before the devaluation of its currency.
   a. standard of living   b. foreign trade   c. gold standard
7. This _____ produces goods in France and the United States.
   a. foreign exchange market   b. European Monetary System   c. multinational corporation
8. Those countries hope to correct their negative balance of trade by _____ more goods.
   a. exporting   b. supporting   c. importing

DEVALUATION

Note: The information contained in the following dialogue is based on articles appearing in *Business Week*, August 10, 1981, p. 80, and in *The New York Times*, October 5, 1981, p. 1.

Jill Connors, an American living in France, and her friend Marie Pottier, a Frenchwoman, are walking through the streets of Paris. Jill notices a long line of people waiting at a foreign exchange office.

Jill   Look at all those people in line, Marie. Why are they waiting at the foreign exchange office?

Marie   There are rumors that the government is going to devalue the franc. I suspect those people are trying to buy German marks or Dutch guilders, which are strong currencies.

Jill   A devaluation! That sounds serious.

Marie   Well, bankers and government officials have been saying lately that a realignment of the exchange rates of the European Monetary System is necessary.

Jill   Why do they think it's necessary to realign European currencies? I would think that since the establishment of the Common Market, economic conditions would be similar in all countries.

Marie   That hasn't yet happened. Inflation rates, for instance, vary greatly. In Germany, inflation is low, about 6% a year, while in Italy it's relatively high, about 20% per year. France is in the middle, with about 13% yearly inflation.

Jill   I imagine that the devaluation will have a considerable effect on foreign trade.

Marie   It will indeed. It should make it easier for France and Italy to export to Germany by making their products less expensive. It will also be more difficult for Frenchmen and Italians to buy imported goods after the devaluation since the price of German and Dutch imports will rise. There is hope that this move will reduce our deficits in the balance of trade.

Jill   But maybe the talk of devaluation is nothing more than a rumor. It's possible that these people are acting too quickly in selling their francs.

Marie   Yes, that's always possible. However, the rumors themselves set off speculation and big investors, such as the multinational corporations, begin exchanging their holdings in weak currencies for marks or dollars, hoping for an upward revaluation of those strong currencies.

Jill   So speculative pressure itself can trigger a devaluation. Interesting. But Marie, isn't some fluctuation normal in the value of a currency?

Marie   Of course. But the EMS was designed to limit the margin of fluctuations. Each country's central bank must buy or sell its currency in foreign exchange markets to keep fluctuations within the specified limits. France has spent billions of dollars of reserves recently to support the franc. The idea behind the EMS was that freely floating currencies can have bad effects on the economy.

Jill What else has the French government been doing to bolster the franc?
Marie The government has kept interest rates at a record high of over 20% to prevent the flight of capital to other countries.
Jill Has this policy been effective?
Marie Well, some people have claimed that the government should restrict monetary expansion. But the government wants to create jobs in the public sector to fight unemployment.
Jill I know that Germany is pursuing a policy in the opposite direction. I guess this means the differential in the rates of inflation will widen.
Marie Most likely. That's why the currency realignment is necessary.
Jill Do you think a return to the gold standard would be helpful?
Marie I'm not sure, although I know many people who think so. I think inflation and the rising price of energy have more to do with problems in the balance of trade.
Jill Well, I guess all we can do is hope that the devaluation will not lower the standard of living.

Comprehension Check

A. State whether each statement is true or false based on the reading passage.

1. People at the foreign exchange office probably want to buy German marks or Dutch guilders.
2. Realignment of European currencies is unnecessary since the Common Market came into being.
3. The standard of living in Common Market countries is more or less the same.
4. The devaluation will make it possible for the French to buy German imports at lower prices.
5. Multinational corporations that acquire dollars or marks hope for an upward revaluation of these strong currencies.
6. The European Monetary System limits the margin of fluctuation in exchange rates among European nations.
7. According to the EMS, allowing the value of a currency to be determined by supply and demand can have bad effects on the economy.
8. France has not attempted to control the flight of capital to other countries.
9. The French government hopes to reduce unemployment through the creation of jobs in government and public corporations.
10. The European currency realignment will certainly widen the differential in the rates of inflation among the participating nations.

B. Answer the following questions orally.

1. What is the purpose of the European Monetary System and who are its members?
2. Why is it necessary to realign European currencies?

3. What will be the effects of the devaluation of the European currencies on foreign trade?
4. What are freely floating currencies?
5. What are the ways in which the French government can bolster the franc?

C. **Composition**. Write a paragraph explaining how the devaluation of currency affects a nation's balance of trade. Refer specifically to some European countries.

Building Your Vocabulary

A. **Matching**. Find the words in the right-hand column that match the words closest in meaning in the left-hand column.

1. public sector
2. put into motion
3. support
4. fuel
5. limit
6. value
7. standard of living
8. realign
9. unemployment
10. increase in money supply

a. level of material life
b. restrict
c. lack of jobs for workers
d. trigger
e. bolster
f. adjust
g. monetary expansion
h. government and public corporations
i. worth
j. energy

B. **Rewriting sentences**. Rewrite each of the following sentences replacing the underlined word or words with the correct form of one of the new words of this lesson.

1. Many European countries have had to consider a change in the value of their currencies.
2. The experts recommend an adjustment of the exchange rates.
3. The government is trying to control monetary expansion.
4. Spain will have to sell more of its goods and services abroad.
5. Government policies should be established to support the guilder.
6. The influence of speculators on the exchange rates set off the devaluation of the German mark.
7. The prices of Dutch goods brought to and sold in Italy will rise.
8. Many of the companies that produce their goods in more than one country have exchanged their holdings in weak currencies for strong ones.

Devaluation   **145**

PRESENTATION

I. Adjective clauses

This is the rumor. *The rumor* set off speculation.
→ This is the rumor *that set off speculation.*

These are the Frenchmen. *They* bought marks.
→ These are the Frenchmen *who bought marks.*

That is the investor. I know *that investor.*
→ That is the investor $\begin{Bmatrix} who\,(m) \\ that \end{Bmatrix}$ I know.
   or
→ That is the investor *I know.*

There's the stock exchange. We visited *it.*
→ There's the stock exchange $\begin{Bmatrix} that \\ which \end{Bmatrix}$ we visited.
   or
→ There's the stock exchange *we visited.*

This is the street. Monique lives *on this street.*
→ This is the street *where Monique lives.*

We will speak to the workers. *The workers'* wages are low.
→ We will speak to the workers *whose wages are low.*

I remember the week. The government announced the devaluation *that week.*

→ I remember the week $\begin{Bmatrix} when \\ that \end{Bmatrix}$ the government announced the devaluation.

II. Infinitives and infinitive phrases with subjects

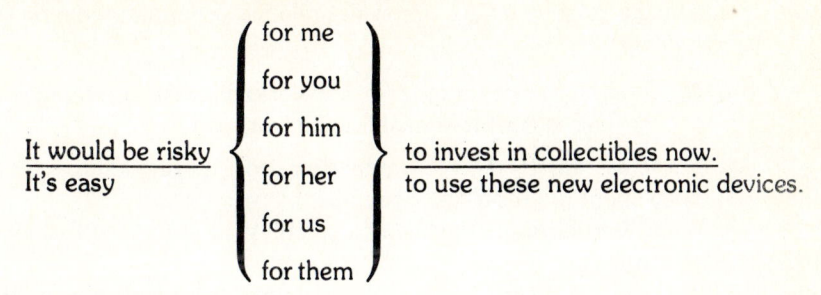

It would be risky / It's easy { for me, for you, for him, for her, for us, for them } to invest in collectibles now. / to use these new electronic devices.

Structure Practice

A. Combine each of the following pairs of sentences into one sentence containing an adjective clause. Introduce the adjective clause with one of these relative pronouns: *that, which, who(m), whose, where, when*.

Model: This is the company. We purchased *its* computer.
→ This is the company whose computer we purchased.

1. These are the European currencies. *They* were devalued.
2. The year was 1981. The government realigned the exchange rates *that year*.
3. There are several big investors. *They* head multinational corporations.
4. Here's the street. The foreign exchange office is *here*.
5. We met the workers. *Their* unemployment rate is very high.
6. I read the new policies. *They* should improve the standard of living.
7. Do you know some of the officials? *They* work for the government.
8. These are the nations. *Their* exports are greater than their imports.
9. The banker was concerned about the interest rates. *They* were limiting the flight of capital.
10. Come with me to the office. The most recent records are kept *there*.

B. Complete each of the following sentences by adding the correct relative pronoun. You will form a paragraph about a visit to a foreign exchange office in France.

1. This is the foreign exchange office _____ we went.
2. It was Tuesday _____ we went there.
3. It was my friend Colette _____ suggested we go.
4. It was Colette _____ had heard the rumor about the devaluation of the franc.
5. There were many people waiting in line _____ purpose in coming was to buy marks or guilders.
6. We brought thousands of francs _____ we wanted to exchange.
7. It was those rumors _____ made so many people anxious to exchange their francs.
8. It was 2 P.M. _____ an official finally called us over.
9. It was at window number 4 _____ we exchanged our francs for marks.

Devaluation

C. Combine each of the following pairs of sentences into one sentence containing a relative clause. Omit the relative pronoun in joining the two sentences.

Model: This is the brokerage firm. He worked for the brokerage firm.
→ This is the brokerage firm he worked for.

1. These are the goods. We wanted to export these goods.
2. They spent the reserves. They had the reserves.
3. We're worried about the unemployment. We have unemployment in our country.
4. We want to return to the gold standard. We used to have the gold standard.
5. Here's the energy report. The committee prepared the energy report.
6. We must find a way to pay for the imports. We need the imports.
7. Here's the multinational corporation. She bought stock in the multinational corporation.
8. Do you know the broker? I consulted the broker.
9. These are the currencies. Speculators are buying the currencies.
10. This is the policy. The European Monetary System follows this policy.

D. Tell about a plan to speculate in currency. Combine each pair of sentences into one sentence containing a relative clause. Give two answers as in the model.

Model: This is the official. I spoke with him.
→ This is the official I spoke with.
or
This is the official with whom I spoke.

1. This is the data. You asked for it.
2. These are the companies. We invested in them.
3. There are the board members. I'll be meeting with them.
4. This is the plan. She talked about it.
5. Here are the figures. They've been looking for them.
6. This is the problem. I looked into it.
7. Here are the German marks. He exchanged the pesetas for them.
8. They have the book. We listed all the entries in it.

E. Restate each of the following sentences using the more common pattern which begins with the word *it*.

Model: To trigger a devaluation is possible.
→ It's possible to trigger a devaluation.

1. To build up the country's reserves is essential.
2. To support the lira is important.
3. To allow the currencies to float is unwise.
4. To control the flight of capital is difficult.

5. To go back to the gold standard is useful.
6. To work for the government is demanding.
7. To raise the standard of living takes time.
8. To fight unemployment is necessary.
9. To study the energy problem is practical.
10. To realign European currencies is serious.

F. Restate each of the following sentences adding the cue in parentheses.

Model: It would be nice to earn more money. (for us)
→ It would be nice for us to earn more money.
1. It would be useful to buy more imported goods. (for you)
2. It would be hard to pay the oil bill. (for them)
3. It would be easy to exchange the francs for dollars. (for her)
4. It would be good to work in the public sector. (for him)
5. It would be better to improve the balance of trade. (for us)
6. It would be preferable to check the value of the guilder. (for you)
7. It would be difficult to lessen the differential in interest rates. (for them)
8. It would be bad to believe the rumors about the devaluation. (for him)

Building Sentences

A. Select elements from columns **A**, **B**, **C** and **D** to form at least ten sentences that have infinitive phrases of the pattern,

It (+ to be) + adjective + interested subject + infinitive phrase
Add any necessary words.

Model: It's difficult for me to exchange these pounds.

	A	B	C	D
It + be	easy	for me	to export	the currency
(any	impossible	for you	to create	a devaluation
tense)	risky	for the officials	to realign	monetary
	difficult	for him	to bolster	expansion
	unfair	for Jill	to import	the gold standard
	wise	for us	to restrict	German marks
	good	for people	to exchange	unemployment
	better	for the	to float	energy
	preferable	government	to trigger	new jobs
	bad	for the banks	to improve	goods
	nice	for them	to devalue	francs
	important	for the public	to realign	standard of living
		sector		Dutch guilders
		for corporations		

Devaluation **149**

B. Complete each of the following sentences by selecting either *a* or *b*.

1. These are the imported goods _____ I was telling you about.
   a. that   b. who
2. Do you know the foreign exchange office _____ we bought the marks?
   a. where   b. which
3. Here's a list of the countries _____ currencies are being devalued.
   a. which   b. whose
4. It's difficult for the government _____ monetary expansion.
   a. to restrict   b. restrict
5. The day _____ they announced the devaluation there were long lines at the foreign exchange office.
   a. where   b. when
6. There are many Italians _____ can no longer afford Dutch imports.
   a. whose   b. who
7. The rise in interest rates is something _____ must be controlled.
   a. which   b. who
8. It would be necessary _____ to work in the public sector.
   a. for them   b. to them
9. This is the multinational corporation _____ he did business.
   a. with which   b. with that
10. Here are the marks _____ we exchanged the kroners for.
    a. (no word needed)   b. who
11. Germany is one of the European nations _____ balance of trade is positive.
    a. whose   b. (no word needed)
12. It was in February _____ inflation reached its peak.
    a. which   b. when

C. Complete each of the following sentences by adding an appropriate phrase. Be sure the sentences make sense.

Model: These are the rumors that . . .
   → These are the rumors that set off the speculation.
      These are the rumors that triggered the devaluation.
      These are the rumors that caused interest rates to rise., etc.

1. These are the goods that . . .
2. Holland is the country where . . .
3. Did you speak to the officials who . . . ?
4. It's important for you to . . .
5. This is the foreign exchange office which . . .
6. It would be impossible for me to . . .
7. Here are the workers whose . . .
8. It's wise for the Common Market to . . .

150

BANKING CONVERSATIONS

A. The European nations are allowing a realignment of the exchange rates.

1. You are a French government official. Discuss what the devaluation of the franc will mean to your nation in terms of imports and exports, balance of trade, inflation, unemployment, the standard of living, etc.
2. You are a German government official. Discuss what the revaluation means to your nation in those terms.

B. You are a citizen of a country whose currency is going to be devalued according to rumors you have heard. Describe your reaction to these rumors and explain what you plan to do in response to them and why.

APPENDIX

I. Cardinal numbers

1	one	11	eleven	21	twenty-one	40	forty
2	two	12	twelve	22	twenty-two	50	fifty
3	three	13	thirteen	23	twenty-three	60	sixty
4	four	14	fourteen	24	twenty-four	70	seventy
5	five	15	fifteen	25	twenty-five	80	eighty
6	six	16	sixteen	26	twenty-six	90	ninety
7	seven	17	seventeen	27	twenty-seven	100	one hundred
8	eight	18	eighteen	28	twenty-eight		
9	nine	19	nineteen	29	twenty-nine		
10	ten	20	twenty	30	thirty		

200	two hundred
300	three hundred
400	four hundred
536	five hundred (and) thirty-six
1,000	one thousand
2,000	two thousand
3,456	three thousand four hundred (and) fifty-six
10,000	ten thousand
20,000	twenty thousand
38,765	thirty-eight thousand seven hundred (and) sixty-five
100,000	one hundred thousand
363,459	three hundred sixty-three thousand four hundred (and) fifty-nine
1,000,000	one million
10,000,000	ten million
268,629,822	two hundred sixty-eight million six hundred twenty-nine thousand eight hundred (and) twenty-two
1,000,000,000	one billion
1,000,000,000,000	one trillion

Notes:

1. English speakers often count by hundreds between 1,100 and 9,999. Thus, 4,950 may be read either "four thousand nine hundred fifty" or "forty-nine hundred fifty."
2. In Great Britain the numeral 1,000,000,000,000 is called a billion rather than a trillion as in the United States. 1,000,000,000 in Great Britain is called one thousand millions.

II. Ordinal numbers

first	1st	twentieth	20th	hundredth	100th
second	2d, 2nd	twenty-first	21st	thousandth	1000th
third	3d, 3rd	twenty-second	22(n)d	millionth	1,000,000th
fourth	4th	twenty-third	23(r)d		
fifth	5th	twenty-fourth	24th		
sixth	6th	twenty-fifth	25th		
seventh	7th	twenty-sixth	26th		
eighth	8th	thirtieth	30th		
ninth	9th	thirty-seventh	37th		
tenth	10th	fortieth	40th		

Ordinal numbers are also used to express fractions: 2/3 = two thirds.
Exceptions: 1/2 = one half; 1/4 = one quarter, one fourth.

III. Dates, days of the week, months of the year

Days of the week	Months of the year	
Sunday	January	July
Monday	February	August
Tuesday	March	September
Wednesday	April	October
Thursday	May	November
Friday	June	December
Saturday		

weekdays—Monday through Friday
weekend—Saturday and Sunday
on Sunday—this coming Sunday   or   last Sunday
on Sundays—every Sunday

Reading years:

1810—eighteen ten (less common: one thousand eight hundred ten)
1876—eighteen seventy-six
1929—nineteen twenty-nine
1978—nineteen seventy-eight

Reading dates:

June 6, 1943—June sixth nineteen forty-three
August 25, 1944—August twenty-fifth nineteen forty-four
July 2, 1967—July second nineteen sixty-seven

VOCABULARY

Notes to Vocabulary

Numbers following each entry refer to the number of the lesson in which the item was introduced. Entries followed by more than one number (e.g., term 3; 10; 13) have been introduced with different meanings in each of the lessons marked. Entries marked (R) are vocabulary items that appear in the supplementary reading activities and are not treated as active vocabulary in this book.

abroad   9
acceptance   8
access   9
accommodate   1
account   1
   charge account   3
   checking account   2
   joint account   1
   N.O.W. account   2
   savings account   1
   term-deposit account   1
   close an account   1
   open an account   1
accounts payable   7
accounts receivable   7
accountant   7
accrual basis   7
accrual system   7
active   11
activity: volume of activity   8
additional   10
address   5 (R)
adjust   4
administer   2
advances   8
advantage   9
agreement   5
alimony   5 (R)
amortization   7
amount: outstanding amount   5
annual   4 (R)

annual report   7
appraisal   6
appreciate   12
art: work of art   12
assets   1
   current assets   1
   fixed assets   1
assign   7
auction   12
audit (*verb*)   6
automatic: automatic teller
      machine   13

balance (*noun*)   2
   minimum balance   2
balance sheet   1
bargain   12
   bargain-hunter   12
basic: basic goods   10
basis: accrual basis   7
   cash basis   7
basis point   9
bear   12
bearish   12
beneficiary   6
bequeath   6
bequest   6
bid (*noun*)   12
bill   13
bill of exchange   8
board of governors   8

155

bolster   14
bond   8
  municipal bond   11
bookkeeping   2
books: to keep the books   2
borrow   3
broker   11
brokerage firm   11
budget   5
bull   12
bullish   12
business day   2 (R)

CAD (computer-aided
    design)   12 (R)
CAM (computer-aided
    manufacture)   12 (R)
cancelled check   2
capacity   5
capital   8
  flight of capital   14
card: charge card   3
cash   5
  cash flow   5
  cash basis   7
  cash system   7
category   7
ceiling   9
certificate   4
  certificate of deposit   4
  stock certificate   8
character   5
charge   2
  service charge   2
  charge account   3
  charge card   3
check   2
  cancelled check   2
  outstanding check   2
  personal check   2
  check-clearing process   13
  check safekeeping   13
  check truncation   13
checking account   2
chute   13 (R)

clear (*verb*)   13
clearance   2 (R)
close: to close an account   1
code: code number   13
coin   12
collateral   3
collectibles   12
co-maker   5 (*see also* co-signer)
commercial   2
  commercial bank   2
  commercial loan   3
  commercial paper   7
commission   12
commitment: loan commitment   10
commodity   11
common: common stock   11
competitive   9
compound: to compound
    interest   2 (R)
compute   3
computer   1
  computer-aided design   12 (R)
  computer-aided
    manufacture   12 (R)
  computer peripherals   12 (R)
consumer: consumer credit   5
control: exchange controls   9
conveyance   4
corporate   9
corporation: multinational
    corporation   14
corrective   10
co-sign   5
co-signer   5
cost: handling costs   13
court: Probate Court   6
credit   5; 7
  consumer credit   5
  installment sales credit   5
  to extend credit   5
credit bureau   5
credit file   3
credit rating   3
credit references   5 (R)
credit standard   10
creditor   3

creditworthy 5
currency 9 (R); 10
currently 3
cycle 2 (R)

daily 2
data 5
data processing 12
dealer 12
debentures 7
debit 7
debt 3
debtor 3
deceased 6
default 3
deficit 10
delay (*noun*) 1
delisted 12 (R)
demand deposit 2
demanding 10
deposit (*noun & verb*) 1
   demand deposit 2
depositor 1
depository 13 (R)
devaluation 10
devalue 10
device 13
differential 14
discount (*verb*) 8
disqualify 5 (R)
distribute 6
dividend 11
double: double-digit 12
Dow Jones Industrial Average 11
down payment 4
downright 13 (R)
draw (up) 6
due 3

earnings 12
economy 10
effect: in effect 3
electronic 13
   electronic funds transfer 13
electronically 13

emerging 12 (R)
empower 8
enclosed 12 (R)
endorse 1
energy 14
enter 7
entry 13
equipment 7
equitable 4 (R)
equity 7
estate: real estate 4
   estate settlement 6
   estate tax 6
   to settle an estate 6
Eurodollar 9
Euromarket 9
European Monetary System 14
exchange 9
   exchange controls 9
   exchange rate 9
   bill of exchange 8
   stock exchange 8
executor 6
expansion: monetary expansion 14
expense 7
export (*verb & noun*) 14
extend: extend credit 6
extension 5 (R)

face up 13 (R)
factor 9
failure 5 (R)
fall (*verb*) 4
far-reaching 13
Federal Deposit Insurance
    Corporation 2 (R)
fee 2
file (*verb*) 6
fill out 1
finance 4
firm 11
fiscal period 7
fixed 4
flexible 4 (R)
flight of capital 14

Vocabulary **157**

float 14
fluctuate 4
foreclose 4
foreign trade 14
format 9 (R)
funds 10
   insufficient funds 2
   mutual fund 11
   uncollected funds 2 (R)
futures 11

goods: basic goods 10
governor: board of governors 8
gross 5 (R)
gross national product 10
growth rate 12
guarantee (*verb*) 4
guaranteed-rate period 4

heir 6
holdings 8
home-free 13 (R)
hourly 2
hunt 12

import (*verb & noun*) 14
impose 10
income 7
increase 10
index 4 (R)
   price index 11
inflation 12
installment 5
   installment plan buying 5
   installment sales credit 5
instant retrieval 13
instrument 4
insufficient funds 2
insurance premium 9
interest 1
international banking facilities 9
International Monetary Fund 10
intervention 8

intestate 6
invest 9
investment 8; 9
investor 9
issue (*noun*) 11; 12 (R)
   back issue 12 (R)
itemize 13

joint account 1
journal 7

keep: to keep the books 2

ledger 7
legacy 6
legatee 6
   residuary legatee 6
lend 3
liabilities 1
life 4
limit (*noun*) 4
liquidity 12
loan 3
   commercial loan 3
   loan agreement 5
   loan application 3
   loan commitment 10
   loan department 3
   mortgage loan 4
   passbook loan 5
   personal loan 3
lobby 7
loss: profit and loss statement 7
lower 4

mailing 13
maintenance: separate
   maintenance 5 (R)
manager 1
mandatory 8
margin requirements 8

market: market price 8
   foreign exchange market 14
maximum 2
membership fee 5 (R)
merger 11
microfilm 13
minimum balance 2
modestly 4 (R)
money supply 4
monitor (*verb*) 4 (R)
monthly 2
monthly statement 2
mortgage 4
   mortgage department 4
   mortgage loan 4
mortgagee 4
mortgagor 4
multinational corporation 14
municipal bond 11
mutual fund 11

name (*verb*) 6
negotiable 2
note: promissory note 7
notification 4 (R)
N.O.W. account 2

occupancy 7
offshore 9
oil 10
  oil-poor 10
  oil-rich 10
onshore 9
open: open an account 1
open market 8
option 4 (R) 12
order (*noun*) 2
oriented: high-technology
    oriented 12 (R)
ounce 12
outstanding 5
  outstanding check 2
overdrawn 2
overseas 9

over-the-counter trading 11
owe 1

paper: commercial paper 7
party 1
pass on 9
passbook 1
passbook loan 5
pay back 3
pay off 3
paycheck 1
payee 2
payment: down payment 4
  stop payment 2
payor 13
penalty 2
per capita 10
peripherals 12 (R)
personal check 2 (R)
point 11
  basis point 9
policy 8; 9
portfolio 11
portion 13 (R)
possession: to take possession of 3
power: purchasing power 2 (R)
preferred stock 11
premises 7
premium: insurance premium 9
previous 5 (R)
price 4
  market price 8
  price-earnings ratio 11 (R)
  price index 11
  purchase price 4
prime 9 (R)
principal 3
probate (*verb*) 6
  Probate Court 6
procedure 13
process (*verb*) 13
processing: data processing 12
product: gross national product 10
profile 5
profit and loss statement 7

Vocabulary **159**

project (*noun*) 10
promissory note 7
property: real property 4
provision 6
public sector 14
purchase (*verb*) 8
purchasing power 2 (R)

quarterly 2

raise (*verb*) 4
range 12 (R)
rate 1
   exchange rate 9
   growth rate 12
ratio 8
real estate 4
real property 4
realign 14
realignment 14
recession 12
record (*noun*) 2; 14
rediscount (*noun*) 8
reduce 13
references: credit references 5 (R)
reform (*noun & verb*) 10
regulate 4 (R)
regulation 9
remove 9
report 7
reporting agency 5
requirement 8
   margin requirements 8
   reserve requirements 8
Reserve Credit 2 (R)
reserves 14
residuary legatee 6
restrict 14
retain 13 (R)
retire 13
retrieval: instant retrieval 13
return (*noun*) 6
revaluation 14
review (*verb*) 4 (R)

rise (*verb*) 4
risk (*noun*) 4
   sovereign risk 9
rounded 4 (R)

safekeeping: check safekeeping 13
salary 13
sales 11 (R)
savings account 1
sector: public 14
security 8
service charge 2
set (*verb*) 8
settle an estate 6
settlement: estate settlement 6
share (*noun*) 10
shelter: tax shelter 11
sign 1
signature 1
slip (*noun*) 1
slowdown 12
social security 13
   social security number 5 (R)
solvent 1
sovereign risk 9
speculate 11
speculation 11
speculative 11
   speculative pressure 14
split 11
spot 9 (R)
spouse 5 (R)
stamp (*noun*) 12
standard 10
   credit standard 10
statement 2
   monthly statement 2
   profit and loss statement 7
station 13 (R)
statistical 12 (R)
stock (*noun*) 8
   stock certificate 8
   stock exchange 8
stockbroker 11
stop payment 2

storage 13
strategy 12
strengthen 10
subject to collection 2 (R)
subscription 12 (R)
subsidiary 9
subtract 2
successful 10
supply: money supply 4
support: child support 5 (R)
support (*verb*) 14
suspicious 10

table 9 (R)
tax 6
   estate tax 6
   tax-exempt 11
   tax shelter 11
taxable 11
technology 13
   high technology 12
teller 1
tenure 3
term(s) 3; 10; 13
   term-deposit account 1
testament 6
testator 6
Third World 10
tight 4
time: on time 5
title 4
trade: balance of trade 14
   foreign trade 14
trading: over-the-counter trading 11
transaction 2

trial 12 (R)
trigger (*verb*) 14
truncation: check truncation 13
trust 6
   trust department 6
   trust fund 6
trustee 6

uncollected funds 2 (R)
unemployment 14
uniform 8
utilities 11

validate 13 (R)
validator 13 (R)
value (*noun*) 14
variable 4
vary 4
version 9 (R)
volume of activity 8

wage 13
weaken 10
weekly 2
will (*noun*) 6
window 1
withdraw 1
withdrawal 1
works of art 12

yearly 2
yield 12

Vocabulary **161**